STUDIES IN COMPARA

The purpose of the collection 'Studie[s in Comparative Politics]' is to provide the students of politics v[ith a series of up-to-date,] short and accessible surveys of the [progress of the discipline,] its changing theoretical approaches and its methodological reappraisals.

The format of the individual volumes is understandably similar. All authors examine the subject by way of a critical survey of the literature on the respective subject, thus providing the reader with an up-to-date *bibliographie raisonnée* (either separate or contained in the text). Each author then proposes his own views on the future orientation. The style tries to bridge the often lamented gap between the highly specialised language of modern political science and the general reader. It is hoped that the entire collection will be of help to the students who try to acquaint themselves with the scholarly perspectives of contemporary politics.

S. E. Finer
Ghiţa Ionescu

A. H. BROWN: Soviet Politics and Political Science
BERNARD CRICK: Basic Forms of Government
C. H. DODD: Political Development
GHIŢA IONESCU: Comparative Communist Politics
DENNIS KAVANAGH: Political Culture
LESLIE J. MACFARLANE: Political Disobedience
W. J. M. MACKENZIE: The Study of Political Science Today
GEOFFREY K. ROBERTS: What is Comparative Politics?
WILLIAM WALLACE: Foreign Policy and the Political Process
ROGER WILLIAMS: Politics and Technology
LESLIE WOLF-PHILLIPS: Comparative Constitutions

STUDIES IN COMPARATIVE POLITICS
published in association with
GOVERNMENT AND OPPOSITION

a quarterly journal of comparative politics, published by Government and Opposition Ltd, London School of Economics and Political Science, Houghton Street, London, WC2 2AE.

Basic Forms of Government

A Sketch and a Model

BERNARD CRICK

Professor of Politics, Birkbeck College, University of London

First edition 1973
Reprinted 1980

Published by
THE MACMILLAN PRESS LTD
London and Basingstoke
Associated companies in Delhi Dublin
Hong Kong Johannesburg Lagos Melbourne
New York Singapore and Tokyo

ISBN 0 333 13753 1

Printed in Hong Kong

CONTENTS

INTRODUCTION

This essay is unlike others in the series in that I have found the division of opinion about forms of government so extreme and the literature so confused that I have abandoned any idea of surveying the major writings on theories and classifications, and have preferred to offer a simple classification of my own based on traditional theories, but in the References at the end have identified the major schools and differences.

In such labour one can either be very brief or very long-winded : I want to be very brief and to write a genuine introduction to stimulate thought about the subject and not simply to offer basic information. There are no such things as facts in the social sciences, there are only concepts which give order to facts. From concepts we construct theories and generalisations which claim that something is the case. Facts must then be adduced, but they can never prove a theory for however many facts are accumulated there is always the possibility of a contrary instance. Facts can only disprove a theory. So we must always start with concepts and theories.

Nothing might seem more dull than to consider forms of government. It is, of course, more important to consider what we as political animals should do. But one must begin with the habit of thinking, which asks not merely if something is desirable, but if it is possible, or possible at what sort of price, with what kind of difficulties. Go to the moon if you wish or try to build New Jerusalem on England's green and pleasant land, but first understand how and at what cost. Forms of government do, indeed, limit our possibilities of action. Anarchists, for that reason, see all forms of government as bad, as limiting the potentialities of the

7

individual. But so does everything: my height, my weight, my age, my attainments and my intelligence allow me to do some things but not others. I admit that I am probably rather unimaginative in making the best or the most of what I have to hand, but one has to start by appreciating the formal constraints. So too with forms of government. They are more numerous than we commonly imagine, particularly when we keep telling ourselves, if we are good social scientists, how unique is the modern world – which is often an excuse for a lazy ignorance about comparative and historical political systems, many of whose features are still to be found in the world today – large parts of which are still stubbornly un-modern. We must beware above all of teleological explanations, that something is happening for a purpose. I shudder with fear every time I come across, for instance, the word 'modernising' or 'modernisation'. It is all right if it simply and openly expresses an *aspiration* to change something, perhaps even in the teeth of circumstances – though it also helps to say what we think 'modern' is, which is then no more than a pretentious way of stating our political doctrines, what we wish to see happen that we believe empirically could happen. But more often 'modernisation' imputes a mysterious process, like Victorian 'Progress', benign and inevitable: so that whole books get written about why Uganda or Ghana or Bolivia is not modernising, books which often leave us with very little information about what factors do in fact condition the politics of the country, actual factors, not concepts thrust on them by either French or German Marxists or American social scientists.

So all I wish to do, as part of an introduction to the study of politics for someone beginning to think about the nature of politics, whether at school, university or perhaps on his own in an evening after work – where most genuine free thought takes place, is to offer firstly, in Part One, a highly simplified sketch of what seem to me to be the main forms of government that men have recognised, and then secondly, in Part Two, an abstract model of what I take to be the three basic systems. For at the highest level of abstraction and theory, the basic forms are few.

Part One, the *Sketch,* is historical and simply identifies and characterises numerous types of regime that people have talked about, irrespective of how much they have in common, and with no attempt at explanation. Part Two, the *Model,* does something

8

different : it seeks to identify basic similarities through all time and circumstance on the basis of apparent coincidences of explanation which follow from identifying the main theories of government. But in this brief compass I do not in any way inquire into the validity of these eleven main theories that lead to the three models, I just introduce them on the tolerant grounds that serious people have taken them seriously; and neither can I set down the evidence, nor all the contrary arguments of hybrids and exceptions, relevant to the sketch of historically perceived types. Let me risk my arm, neck or judgement : concepts must be established and theories stated before their utility and validity, respectively, can be fully established. I stop short at that point deliberately : for to go beyond it is, I still hope or fear, a major work for one's last years of vigour – in which I have now interrupted myself for several years to write George Orwell's biography. So I am happy to offer something seemingly dogmatic, but rather with the flavour of 'work in progress', something with a built-in obsolescence, to be modified or even torn to pieces without too great a loss.

Part Two of this essay appeared first in *Government and Opposition*, Volume 3, Number 1, Winter 1968, though now with some minor revisions and one additional theory (I now see that 'property' has been used to define types of government in a sense more specific than 'economy'), and I thank the editors of the present series for remorselessly nagging me into revising and expanding it. This second part I worked out in lectures at Sheffield on Historical Political Systems, trying to bridge the awful gap between the History of Political Thought and Comparative Political Systems – the first of which rarely contains anything about thoughts on political organisation, only on ethics; and second of which is usually only comparative in the most foolishly contemporary and short-term way, lacking in any historical depth. Personally, I think our subject will only achieve coherence if it is taught as an account of the political factors involved in the rise and fall, change or decay, of different types of society, only here do 'ideas' and 'institutions' and the 'normative' and the 'positive' cease to pull apart and pull together. I would thank my former Sheffield students for criticism of Part Two, and would hope that Part One may also prove useful in sixth forms, if better syllabuses ever come.

B. R. C.

A Sketch of Historical Political Systems

1. PRIMITIVE GOVERNMENT

'Primitive Government' can mean two quite different things : either the earliest, the original or the most simple forms of government, or those elementary, elemental, basic or 'primitive' aspects of all governments even in advanced and complex societies. Since the seventeenth century in Europe, some philosophers like Montesquieu, Hobbes and Locke have had the idea that by studying actual primitive governments we could understand better what is basic and common to all governments. But primitive societies are seldom literate and rarely keep records, so the only primitive societies we have any accurate knowledge of, as distinct from speculations about, are those which have survived into the modern world and have been studied by anthropologists.

Radcliffe-Brown in his book *African Political Systems*,[1] says that government is 'that part of the total organisation which is concerned with the maintenance or establishment of social order, within a territorial framework, by the organised exercise of coercive authority through the use, or the possibility of use, of physical force'. Thus 'order' is seen as a basic characteristic; but note that it may be maintained by the 'possibility' of force, not always its actual use. No government can rest simply on coercive power unless that power is used to establish moral authority. Note also that to mention 'a territorial framework' neither implies necessarily a geographically fixed framework – there have been and are nomadic peoples as well as sedentary, nor does it imply complete independence or autarchy. Most governments are limited in their power by the existence of other governments having external influence, and are also dependent on some foreign trade. Malinowski

11

in his *Scientific Theory of Culture* assumed that government arises also to deal with internal differences: 'Political organisation implies always a central authority with the power to administer regarding its subjects, that is to co-ordinate the activities of the component groups . . .'.[2]

Government is also a response to man's uniquely long period of maturation compared to other animals. Hence the need for continuous protection of children and women of child-bearing age, and the great survival-value of extended kinship, of 'the family' seen as a large but related social group. Primitive governments can then be identified as the government of tribal societies: human communities developed by an association of, and an inter-breeding between, a small number of families, opposed in principle to cross-breeding with other communities and preserving their own customs, beliefs and organisation. This is primal or primitive but we will see that aspects of this also exist in feudal and in aristocratically governed societies.

The control of food supplies is as important as the protection of the family and the maintenance of order. Pastoral societies have usually developed more complex forms of government and a greater division of labour (of which government itself is a specialised function), and they thus tend to survive longer than most nomadic societies. The invention of agriculture implies collective decision-making, some ability to predict the seasons, to store grain and to organise mutual defence of fields and of water supplies.

Are there societies without government at all? Many of the philosophers thought so who speculated about this before the anthropologists could study these matters scientifically. Anarchy can be seen as simplicity and spontaneity, not as confusion and violence: many early Christian philosophers believed that government did not exist before the Fall of Man brought sin into the world; Locke believed that government only followed disputes about ownership and boundaries of property, and was only marginally needed as an 'Umpire'; and Rousseau claimed that so-called 'civilised institutions' had corrupted the natural simplicity of man. But in fact only a very few societies exist with government so minimal as to raise this question seriously; some of the Neur peoples of East Africa, the Eskimo, the Australian aborigines and the Hopi Indians of Arizona.[3] They have no

12

organisation which controls or monopolises violence, or which can enforce laws. But their survival appears to have depended on extreme isolation and extreme simplicity of culture and technology: plainly governments grow more complex in proportion to the internal and external challenges they face – if they are to survive. Government enables societies to adapt to changing conditions.

Personal physical dominance by a chieftain or hero is only possible in the smallest groups; and any society of more than twenty to thirty warriors which aims at perpetuating itself (that is to say not just as a temporary, marauding band), is involved in seeking some degree of self-sufficiency or autarchy which, in turn, involves regular control and consultative administration (not spasmodic plunder) of fields, hunting grounds, mines and sources of water.[4] Thus it appears true that all power does indeed rest on *some kind* of consent. Rulers depend upon agents of all kinds; agents and subjects depend upon rulers – their mutual dependence and antipathy constitute politics.

Mythology often underlines the isolation and vulnerability of kings and chieftains as well as the benefits they bring and their power. The Nordic sagas commonly saw sleep as the fatal flaw of heroes; even Siegfried and Beowulf must sleep and are then utterly dependent on the loyalty (*Treue*) of their men (who may be corrupted) or, failing them, of their dogs sleeping around them (who may be poisoned). The Hebraic myths add women to sleep as the bane of war-lords: Holofernes, the Babylonian general, is beheaded in his sleep by seductive Judith, treacherous Jael drives a tent-peg through the skull of her Philistine lover, and even Samson had his Delilah. So in primitive societies great stress must be put on personal loyalty and oath-taking. Even when the king is cruel, mad, old or incompetent, loyalty is due to him – even to the death, as the saga writers liked us to believe. Rulers in such societies everywhere encourage such impractical views, simply because of the vulnerability and precariousness of power based purely on personal attainments.

The matter is even more complicated if rulers aspire to be kings, that is, to have some say either in choosing their successor, or in knowing that the elders or heads of other clans will choose a successor dynastically – that is, from their own immediate family. Kings must have a following who are loyal

13

to their leader, and they will invariably try to put this loyalty on a supernatural footing. If they themselves are not gods, then they are the chosen spokesmen of gods, or descendants of the great hero or demi-god who, almost invariably in mythology, founded the community. The weakness of primitive societies more often lies in the lack of strong leadership rather than in its excess. Many primitive societies are 'acephalous' – they have no clear head.[5] Elaborate consultation by elders is more typical than sudden decisions by war chiefs or ritual kings. Even where kings appear absolute, the problem of the succession usually limits power or maximises instability – neither customs of descent of nomination nor election work smoothly. As the anthropologist Max Gluckman has observed, 'clear and simple rules indicating a single prince as the true heir' are in fact rare throughout the world.[6] Thus most stable primitive societies tend to be small; only extremely intimate, loyal, traditional and tribal societies can solve these problems of succession and continuity without elaborate constitutional rules.

2. EARLY EMPIRES

The Egyptians, as far as we know, invented the imperial state. The huge oasis of the Delta and then of the Nile valley, linked together by irrigation canals, invited unification. By about 2850 B.C., a centralised and bureaucratic regime controlled this whole area.[7]

At about the same time, there were numerous city states in Sumeria which had reached a high level of culture, even before an attempt was made by the ruler of one of them to achieve hegemony over the rest. Lugalzagessi of Uma – the first name of an emperor we know – had inscribed on stone that he would 'water the whole earth with joy while monarchs lay before him like cattle'. But he was overthrown by Sargon of Akkad, who had a superior military technology of archers instead of chariots and spearsmen, and who boasted of 'conquering thirty chiefs'.

The Akkadian Empire was succeeded by the Babylonian Empire with its codified and published laws. The Hittites flourished until the Assyrians proved even greater empire builders with their disciplined cavalry and firm rules for administration and tax-gathering. The longest lasting ancient empire was that of the Persians, who, on conquering Egypt, took over from the Pharaohs ideas and practices of divine kingship.

The political problem of empires is everywhere the same. How can an alien minority effectively claim permanent authority over peoples of quite different cultures? Pure military coercion can only create an Empire, not perpetuate it – as the Hittites must have discovered. Power can most easily be transmuted into

15

authority when rulers and ruled are not alien but share the same culture or, in the modern world, think of themselves as one nation. But empire is the rule of one culture over others. Imperial authority inherits divisions of interests and tries to manage them, rather than deliberately creating them. Empires rarely try to assimilate their conquered subjects, or only a chosen few of the most able. They are distinct from 'conquest kingdoms' who, driven by plunder or migration, either wipe out or drive away the conquered. The ancient empires invariably utilised slaves, but it is highly doubtful if Marx's sweeping generalisation is invariably correct, that they were dependent on slave power. For one thing, slaves were sometimes used predominantly for domestic purposes and not in the fields, mines and ditches; and for another, conquering empires rarely, if ever, enslaved whole populations. Conquered populations had no rights, but they did not become the personal property of individuals, only subjects of the Emperor or the state – a condition sometimes as bad or worse than that of slavery, but different nonetheless.

To claim simply to be culturally and educationally superior is an insufficient basis for permanent domination – for that would admit a gradual surrender of power if the subject peoples make progress (as in modern colonial empires). So the general solution evolved was everywhere the same, authority was put on an absolute and transcendent basis : rulers were held up as part of, or as representing, the divine order of the universe. Such a claim is unchallengeable if believed to be true. Alexander of Macedon, in conquering the free Greek cities, the Persians and the rest of the known civilised world, had to claim descent from the High God as his only possible claim for legitimacy over peoples with such varying ideas and practices of authority.

The god of empires, however, unlike the local gods of primitive society, claimed an absolute and universal domination over all other gods : in polytheistic cultures, they would claim to be the High Gods. He could even be thought to be, the Persians claimed, the only god : monotheism was a powerful political device. And this universalism corresponded to the experience of the inhabitants. We live in a world of nation states. However fiercely nationalistic we may be, we are always aware that other people do things in very different ways, perhaps not agreeable to us, but

16

at least tolerable. Although we know every part of our planet, we recognise great differences of ideology. But the inhabitants of a vast imperial regime would have no such knowledge and, in so far as they were dimly aware of other regimes, would regard them as barbarians or primitives – people waiting to be taken into the one and only law, or else incapable of ever receiving it. Thus all empires claimed and believed that they had, as the Chinese said, 'the mandate of heaven' to govern the world; the sun would never set on their boundaries, and they hoped to endure for ever.[8]

Empires, aspiring to permanence and universality, are then involved in regular administration: the economic advantages become apparent of continuous exploitation and tax-gathering, rather than 'eating up the land' or sporadic plunder and irregular tribute. Hence the birth of bureaucracy: servants of the ruler or state who hold office by virtue of their administrative skills, not because of their social standing or military power. War-chiefs and tyrants may live for the moment, but imperial-bureaucratic regimes are often content to let sleeping dogs lie and shrewd enough to feed the goose that lays the golden egg. They help create continuity and stability, even at times when the ruler himself is weak or the succession in dispute.

Universal empires are, however, in fact highly artificial forms.[9] There is an inherent strangeness and difficulty in governing vast numbers of distant and alien people on a permanent basis, and in emperors believing or pretending to believe that they are in close touch with the gods or that they are gods. Being artificial and something wholly imposed from without, imperial authorities tended to copy each other's elaborate ceremonials and rituals. Always a vast distance between rulers and subjects had to be stressed and increased in court etiquette – wholly unlike the sweaty intimacy between rulers and ruled in both primitive societies and city states. *Prostrasis* was an almost universal institution – grovelling in the dust before the ruler, the honour due to gods, rather than the simple bow or nod of one man to another.[10] Alexander forced it on the Greeks to whom as free men it was utter degradation. Rarely did the emperor appear on the same physical level as his subjects; often he is so divine that he does not appear in public at all, except at great religious or state festivals, and this can be a sign that rule has been taken over

17

by the palace bureaucracy simply using the name of the emperor – as was the case in Japan[11] and in many parts of the Arab world. The home of the emperor and the bureaucracy is invariably a palace or court constructed on an awe-inspiring and god-like scale of size and magnificence – built to create the illusion of omnipotence rather than to give the grimly practical security for the ruler of the European medieval castles. For, unlike in feudal kingdoms, in lone empires there were and are no rival armies – only the assassin is feared, so hand-picked royal guards are always close and politically important.

Ruling over vast distances involved continual danger of fragmentation. Provincial governors, even if sons of the emperor, tried to set themselves up as local kings or to seize the throne itself. Emperors strove to reward their bureaucrats and generals without letting them bequeath and inherit land, thus becoming semi-independent locally and gaining dynastic or family ambitions. In all early empires, the emperors tried, with varying success, to assert their own nominal ownership of all land, to prevent the automatic inheritance of fixed possessions; but in practice it was often dangerous to disturb the customary rights of great vassals.[12] One solution to the problem of rivalry, adopted in empires as different as Egypt and China, was the employment of eunuchs.[13] Emperors made eunuchs favourite counsellors, provincial governors and even – in Byzantium – generals, to free themselves from the fear that their servants would create rival dynasties. For where there is substantial local autonomy and the inheritance of land and even office, imperial authority declines and the stage is set for feudalism as in both Europe and Japan. Empires thus begin in conquest and are based upon division, not on a single cultural unity. The claims of emperors to be gods become increasingly implausible. When the centre cannot hold, things fall apart. Imperial rule, like liberty, calls for 'eternal vigilance' and restless activity. When armed contests for power immobilise the central palace, the provinces revolt or simply govern themselves. It speaks much for human ingenuity and skill in government that so many empires have lasted so long.

18

3. THE GREEK CITIES

There happened to grow up over a far wider area than modern Greece a civilisation with a common language and culture of men who called themselves Hellenes, but which was divided into many different *polis*. From *polis* come words like 'politics' and 'political', but *polis* itself is hard to translate – perhaps 'polity' comes nearest, but the word is archaic and pompous sounding.[14] 'City-state' is perhaps the best we can do, for even though the majority of citizens would have lived outside the walls or boundaries of the actual city, the city itself dominated the rural areas. But *polis* also implies community, and not merely an independent community but communal government. It is easy for us to accept that tyrants can rule city-states, as in parts of the Moslem world and in Renaissance Italy. But to the Hellene, the very language implied that there was something unnatural and unstable in one man governing a *polis*.

Sophocles made this point in his *Antigone*. Antigone is trying to bury her rebel brother; the tyrant forbids it, and another brother argues with him :

CREON : Then she is not breaking the law ?
HAEMON : Your fellow citizens would deny it to a man.
CREON : And the *polis* proposes to teach me how to rule ?
HAEMON : Ah. Who is it that's talking like a boy now ?
CREON : Can any voice but mine give orders in this *polis* ?
HAEMON : It is no *polis* if it takes orders from one voice.
CREON : But custom gives possession to the ruler.
HAEMON : You'd rule a desert beautifully alone.[15]

And Aristotle did not regard tyranny as a political relation-ship at all : politics, or the government of the *polis*, to him must always involve interaction between citizens. By the time of the great fifth century, most Greeks believed that they had always been governed in this way : they had lost all practical memory of the kings or chiefs of the Homeric era, unlike the Roman republicans who cherished the history or myth that would-be citizens had deliberately chased out the Tarquins, their early kings.

The citizens, of course, were never the majority even of the adult population. There were the women (who never did go on sexual strike until the men stopped fighting, as Aristophanes imagined in his play, *Lysistrata*); there were the slaves (mainly domestic, rarely used *en masse* for public works as in the Middle Eastern empires and later in Rome); there were many foreigners resident in the city, and there were often free-men who were not yet full citizens. M. I. Finley has estimated that the Athenian population numbered at its peak, just before the disastrous Peloponnesian War in 431 B.C., about 250,000 in all – of whom about 40,000 were citizens.[16] But Athens was both the largest and exceptionally large; Thebes, Argos, Corcyra and Acragas were of the order of 40–60,000 inhabitants, and many were far smaller, including Sparta who could never muster more than 5000 men under arms (a relevant measure for times when citizenship was closely tied to the right, duty, skill and economic ability to possess and use arms).

In states of this size it is obvious that there is an intimacy and closeness between citizens, even between rulers and ruled when aristocracies predominated, very different from the vast social and physical distance actually existing and always deliberately extended in the imperial states. Rulers could not pose as gods. Even tyrants had to be somewhat political, had to exhibit the common touch rather than imperiousness, had themselves to play the demagogue, living as they did in sweaty intimacy with their subjects or fellow citizens – in what some have well called 'face-to-face societies'. They jostled shoulder to shoulder in the streets, met and saw each other closely and constantly in the temples, the theatre, the stadium and in the *Agora* (the assembly square in every city where all citizens could gather, which was usually also the market place). If only rarely was a *polis* fully democratic, yet the governing class in all of them, because of their small size and compactness, had to pay realistic respect to the democratic element in their politics. 'It is the *demos*', wrote an anonymous oligarchical pamphleteer, 'which rows the galleys and gives the state its power' – and 'demos', depending on context, meant either 'mob' and a perjorative 'lower-classes', or else 'the people as a whole'.[16]

Not merely were the city-states of Greece small, but Greeks justified smallness of scale. Aristotle said that a state could be neither just nor stable if it was either too large for citizens to know each other's characters, or for the voice of the *stentor*, the herald or the town-crier, to be heard from one side of the city to the other. That everyone should know what was going on seemed to him quite as important as that decisions should be taken by representatives of the people – particularly when the Greeks believed that only direct representation was democratic and that voting for others was inherently oligarchical – for only the best or the richest get elected, not the typical man. If numbers were too large for direct assemblies, they preferred choice by lot – as in a modern jury system. Long centuries afterwards, whenever democratic ideas became plausible again, men worried that there were severe limits of scale on self-government. Rousseau and many of the Jacobins thought that free and popular government was only possible in cities or small states, and this theory animated many of those Americans who in 1787 wanted all real power to lie with the thirteen separate states.[17] But they missed the second dimension of Aristotle's argument: communication was as important as participation, so what if modern technology could amplify 'the voice of the *stentor*'?

In Athens in the fifth century the general assembly, the *Ecclesia* – which all citizens could attend, met about forty times a year. From them an executive council of 500, the *Boule*, was chosen by lot, not by election, and for one year only; and they in turn constituted by rotation an inner council of 50. They nominated a 'Head of State' to make urgent decisions; but he was really only a 'duty officer of the day', for it was a different person every day. There were many officials, but they too were mainly chosen by lot and for short periods. There was thus no bureaucratic class or profession and little or no delegation of authority to elected representatives.

21

Aristotle had assumed that election was an aristocratic or oligarchic device (the wisest, the most powerful or the most wealthy would get elected) and that lottery was the democratic way of appointing magistrates and officials. He himself did not favour so direct a democracy, but praised Solon's alleged original laws of Athens which allowed the people the right of electing magistrates and officials and of calling them to account, but not of holding office themselves.

The one elective element was the *Strategoi*, the board of ten generals, who were voted upon by the assembly. Here, plainly, skill was required more than representativeness. If all this seems an odd logic, consider why we today think it right to select juries at random (wanting average common sense), but to select members of legislatures by competitive voting (since we want them to be at least somewhat skilled or able, not simply typical).

* * *

In fact, in the Hellenic city-states there was a great variation of practice, procedures and intention : some states were professedly oligarchic, some democratic, some vacillated somewhere in between, but all regarded their constitutions as fixed. The city was its laws. If you changed the Athenian laws, you would become something else, Sparta perhaps; if you wanted a Spartan constitution, then go to Sparta. Laws did, of course, change by interpretation and by the erosions and accretions of time; but in all the ancient world it was hard for ordinary men to recognise that new laws could be made – only gods or demi-gods could do that. The idea of making law by statute is modern.

But, nonetheless, it was impossible to live in a small city-state without realising that men did things differently, and yet respectably and reasonably effectively, elsewhere. A certain sense of relativity and a limited secularism permeated Greek thought and experience. They invented political philosophy : the view that there is a distinction between law and justice, that the gods have left men astonishingly free to settle their social relationships between themselves and that this can be done justly by human reason.[18] But of almost equal importance for the whole subsequent Western tradition of politics was the simple example and memory that men had once governed themselves freely in cities – 'ruling and being ruled in turn'.

The Greeks came to recognise that the coexistence of different interests and ideas even within the same *polis* was natural. Aristotle even said that if a *polis* was to advance too much towards moral unity, it would cease to be a *polis* or political community at all and would become a tyranny – an explicit criticism of his master, Plato. In Aristotle's book, *The Politics*, three kinds of government are recognised as being, in the appropriate circumstances, just and stable : monarchy, aristocracy and what he simply called 'polity'. Monarchy was rare or unknown, for it would be only appropriate if there were a perfectly good man – which was to say, a god. In fact, rule by one man is always tyranny : government by one man in his own interest, not to the common good. Aristocracy was the rule of the few on the claim that they were experienced, skilled or wise (*'aristoi'* meaning wisdom or excellence). This was a possible if difficult form of government in the general interest, but too often it becomes corrupted into oligarchy, the rule of the powerful, or plutocracy, the rule of the rich. Democracy, however, while it is the rule of the many (which also means the poor), is a corrupt form of 'polity', for the justification of democracy is the belief 'that because men are equal in some things, they are equal in all' – which Aristotle regards as a fallacy. What then was 'polity' itself ? It was a mixture of aristocracy and democracy : the rule of the wise with the consent of the people and power of the people behind them. But good government is seldom if ever pure democracy. So many textbooks get this wrong, out of ideology or ignorance, that a diagram may help. (See next page.)

Aristotle thought that all stable states were a mixture of these elements : a 'golden mean' was to be sought for, not transcendent righteousness. Philosophy stands in judgement on politics, but it is not itself politics, and philosophers should not seek to be kings – as his own teacher, Plato, had argued, nor are they well fitted to be good statesmen. If circumstances inclined to a harsh political choice between oligarchy and democracy, he inclines to democracy; but in no sense was he simply democratic, nor did his theories lead him to believe that purely democratic states would last for long.

Obviously the city-states, with no bureaucracy, few permanent

23

Aristotle classified regimes according to three different principles and found three types, each with typical degenerations from the ideal form.

	NUMBERS	THE IDEAL (or the moral doctrine)	SOCIAL COMPOSITION
MONARCHY	One man	Perfect rule. If a perfectly just and rational ruler could be found, make him king (therefore very unlikely in practice, for a perfectly just man would be a demi-god; more often one-man rule is simply TYRANNY, rule of one man in his own interest)	One-man rule would stand above normal social relationships – he says 'the man who can live outside the *polis* [the political relationship] is either a beast or a God'
ARISTOCRACY	A few, a minority	Rule of an elite, literally from the Greek *aristoi*, the rule of the wise or the skilled in the general interest, thus the rule of *knowledge* (with the danger of degenerating into PLUTOCRACY, rule of the rich or OLIGARCHY, rule of the strong)	Property owners with leisure, i.e. property, in order to give leisure which is necessary for the attainment of knowledge (and the poor as subjects, not citizens)
DEMOCRACY	The many, the majority	The rule of (mere) *opinion* ('the democrat believes that because men are equal in some things they are equal in all')	The poor monopolising citizenship
POLITY (i.e. all 'single element' systems tend to instability; polity as the best possible government is a mixture of elements)	The few ruling with the active consent of the many (ideally 'ruling and being ruled in turn'). All are fit to choose, but not all to govern	'Mixed government' and 'the middle way', i.e. the aristocratic principle of knowledge creatively blended with the democratic principle of power, the power that comes from participation, mutual knowledge and consent	No great extremes of wealth – the existence of a large middle-class, a citizen culture

ARISTOCRACY — fuse together into — DEMOCRACY — POLITY

leaders, and most of their offices either elective or chosen by lot, would have been highly unstable (or, in some cases, even more so than they were) if there had not been an extraordinary dedication to public business by the citizen class. The Greeks in fact believed that citizenship was the highest end of man, and that the names and memories that would live for ever would be those of great statesmen. The highest object of life was to achieve such immortality. 'Virtue' or *arete* was seen as a blending of thought and action: either was worthless without the other. Homer had described Achilles as a 'doer of deeds and a speaker of words', and gave him Centaur as tutor: someone half-man and half-beast, that is half reason and half compulsive energy. Thus our modern liberal ideas of rights against the state, or of liberty as being left alone from politics, were unknown to the Greeks: a rational and active man was worthy of the right to be a citizen *in order* to share in the common duties of self-government.

When Aristotle in the Fifth Book of his *Politics* gives purely academic advice to tyrants about what they must do in order to perpetuate themselves, he identifies 'high spirit' (*arete*) and 'mutual trust' as being the two things that tyrants must crush utterly – and conversely that which free states must nurture. The man of high spirit must be 'lopped off' before he does anything, just as even, or especially, those non-political social groups which give man the habit of mutual trust which is inimicable to both personal tyranny and collective despotism. While men act as men should, tyranny is an almost impossible business, unless the tyrant goes to such extraordinary and inhuman lengths. He could never (or should never?) count on apathy or widespread feelings of utter hopelessness about rebellion. Tyranny is that abuse of good government which depends entirely on the will-power and success of one man – hence it is nearly always small scale and personal, unlike the large numbers controlled impersonally by the bureaucracies of despotisms.

In fact constant instability of government plagued the Greek world. The great Peloponnesian War between Athens and her allies and Sparta and hers fermented internal struggles between democratic and aristocratic factions in many or most of the cities – often grim and bloody class war, as is retailed in the terrible dispassionate pages of Thucydides. And revolutions did not provide lasting solutions to the violent uncertainty. Indeed to translate

25

the Greek *stasis* as 'revolution' is misleading.[19] For *stasis* was chronic instability, the violent seizure of power by one faction, which led in turn to the other faction striking back : the *demos* usually found its leaders in aggrieved or power-hungry aristocrats, so democratic victories usually led to tyranny. There was much of the tyrant in Pericles, the great Athenian war-time leader, despite the noble, perhaps glib, Periclean oration on self-government. Thus the *stasis* of Greek politics was more like the reality of Latin American and West African politics today than the modern revolutionary ideal of vast and permanent changes for the better, so often preached, so seldom attempted, so rarely achieved.

Their lack of internal unity brought the city-states down before the armies of Macedonia at the battle of Chaeronea in 338 B.C. 'If all the Greeks could join together in one *polis*, they would conquer the world', it was said; but both their institutions and their ideas precluded unity, and made military alliances usually come too little and too late. 'The man who can dwell outside the *polis*', said Aristotle, perhaps thinking of his former pupil, Alexander, 'is either a beast or a god.' Alexander created an empire by aping the god; it fragmented at his death, but the new kingdoms spread Hellenic culture and ideas over the whole known world – cut off, however, from the old basis of their power and pride, communal politics. Macedonia waned and Rome came, Greece was conquered yet again, but the Roman poet Horace wrote : 'Captive Greece may captive her rude conquerer' – an elegant half-truth.

4. REPUBLICAN ROME

Rome was a small city that became an empire – indeed to subsequent history, the Empire. Even after the Republic came to be governed by emperors and no longer by a senate, the legal code continued and brought, over a vast area of the world, justice and peace. These are both relative terms, but their meaning was obvious when a trader could go his way, if he cared, from Syria to Britain or from the Atlas mountains to the Danube without fear of anything more than disease, discomfort and petty theft.

It was no idle boast for Pliny the elder to speak of *immensa Romanae pacis majestas* – 'the measureless majesty of the Roman peace', or simply the *Pax Romana*. Even after 'Eternal Rome' had been sacked by the Goths in A.D. 410 and the political unity of Europe and the Mediterranean destroyed for ever afterwards, the memory and influence of Roman law and of the practices of citizenship lingered on. And in the Eastern Empire, of which Constantine had made Byzantium the capital in A.D. 330, the end did not come until the fall of Constantinople to the Turks in 1453.

Essentially the Republic was government by a tough and imperious aristocracy, but in such circumstances that they needed the active support of 'the people', not just their passive indifference. The circumstances were primarily military, though they may originally have gained constitutional status by the deliberate alliance of the Patrician class with the Plebeians to replace an Etruscan dynasty of monarchs. Military technology and citizenship were closely related.[20] The Romans mainly fought on foot but developed highly elaborate tactics and manoeuvres which

27

demanded both intense collective discipline and high individual skill. The aristocrats were officers who fought with the men, not a warrior caste set apart on horseback; and the common soldiers were craftsmen, not badly armed peasants relying on weight of numbers. It is hard to tell which is cause and which is effect – either the people had to be or could be trusted with arms. The aristocracy had to remain at least to that degree popular. The army and the city mob of Rome itself had to be integrated into the political community. The long and desperate war against Carthage finally cemented this alliance and made the Romans see it, in their histories, as the key to their power : 'mixed government', neither solely aristocratic nor solely democratic.

This mixture of patriotic civil rights and harsh aristocratic realism was tersely asserted on the ensigns of the legions and stamped on all state property : 'S.P.Q.R.', *Senatus Populusque Romani* – The Senate and the People of Rome : this union was the basis of their power over other nations. Cicero simply re-states this common formula in his famous *'Auctoritas in Senatum Potestas in Populum'*. *'Auctoritas'* was, in Sir Frank Adcock's words, 'a mixture of prestige and initiative', and it was to be wielded by the Senatorial class, but to do so effectively they must recognise the ultimate power of the people to make or to break.[21]

The main constitutional device for this was the institution of the Tribunes who were magistrates elected by the Plebeians. In the early Republic they gained authority from actual meetings of the people in a democratic assembly, the *Concilium*, but later the assemblies ceased to meet, and even the elections by the people were limited to candidates of the Senatorial class. But they had a power of veto. It was recognised that no commands of the Senate were constitutionally proper or likely to be effective in fact unless they could carry the people with them. So the aristocrats who sought elections as Tribunes had to be or to play the demagogue. Their power was ordinarily limited to a single annual term of office, but this was sometimes set aside.

The Consuls were also annual officers, but during that time they could apply the entire authority of the Senate which, in turn, limited others in public law but knew no limits itself : they exercised the 'imperium' of the former kings, or the collective power of the whole state. While citizens were protected by known laws and a reasonably impartial judicial system, *imperium* could override all. *'Imperium'* or absolute authority did not cease when the Tarquins were chased out, but was wielded for the whole community by the Senate with the veto of the Tribunes – particularly in foreign policy, which was felt to be a Senatorial matter and not subject, with some famous exceptions, to popular control. Thus the Roman constitution was, in very broad terms, closer to the eighteenth century British idea of the sovereignty of Parliament rather than the American idea of legal restraints upon the Assembly or Congress.

'Imperium' as a shared cultural value carried with it not just authority plus power (limited only by political prudence) within Rome, but an absolute assertion of external authority over others : the states they defeated or who sought their dangerous protection. *'Imperium'* was also a certain self-confidence or arrogance that the Romans were as famous for as their justice. The leaders of Russia and America today furnish psychological parallels. Economic factors condition the basic divisions of power in a society, but how that power is actually used depends most often on astonishingly independent patterns of values. *'Dignitas'*, for instance, was the personal value most prized and cultivated by the Patrician or Senatorial classes; but every commoner also had his *'libertas'* and was expected to assert and exercise it actively. *Dignitas* was the quality that marks out a great man from a small, but the *libertas* of the small man was freedom to do what the law allowed him to do, free from arbitary interventions, and not to suffer more than the law allowed him to suffer. Both were adhered to with equal tenacity. Livy describes a Roman gentleman of the old school as being 'as mindful of the *libertas* of others as he was of his own *dignitas*'.

The keen realism of the Romans about the relationships between power and consent reached its height in the office of *'Dictator'*, for dictatorship was a constitutional office. A man (or two men in early practice) had the unfettered *imperium* surrendered to him for the period of an emergency. If he attempted either to continue in office after an emergency was over or to prolong the emergency artificially in order to retain power, he was *ipso facto* an outlaw – any man could, indeed should, kill him : tyrannicide was the most extreme but the greatest political virtue – the Brutus who killed the last King and the Brutus who killed the first Caesar were equally honoured in re-

29

publican writings. This was hardly a self-correcting mechanism, but it did vividly show the almost desperate intensity with which the Romans pursued two sometimes incompatible values : survival and freedom.

Roman government thus involved both a highly complex set of institutions and a most elaborate and rationalised set of values – the latter consciously taught, analysed, lauded and perpetuated in schools, in literature and in history. That Rome, even of the Republic, could become an empire without, for that reason, losing her internal freedoms was due to a way of looking at these very values that was revolutionary in the ancient world. The 'Roman way of life' could, they believed, be learned and adopted by foreigners. It did not depend on the ethnic composition of the original citizens, nor on the blessing and protection of a set of gods who would only work for their own city. The Romans actually professed to believe that while their city had had an heroic founder, pious Aeneas fleeing from Troy, his successors had gathered followers by making the city a refuge for outlaws and exiles – men having different gods. Despite their rigid class structure, this tough-minded respect for ability rather than birth or descent was engrained right at the heart of the myths that gave the Romans their sense of identity.[22]

The separation of citizenship from race and from the divine protection of local gods was to have momentous consequences. The Romans could extend citizenship to allies or even to the pacified elite of conquered nations. The Romans broke from the severe limits of scale imposed by Greek culture and values on political organisation. Loyalty was due not to 'our noble ancestors' or 'the gods' but to the ideas of the Republic itself. It was thus a culture more dominated by law and politics than was even the Greek.

30

5. IMPERIAL ROME

Polybius described the Roman constitution as 'the Senate proposing, the people resolving, and the magistrates executing the laws.' To the extent to which it was a conscious agreement to respect a mixture of elements as superior and more viable than any one, there was a constant tendency to instability only mitigated by the political skill of the Patrician class. The violence of conflicts of faction and of class rocked the boat dangerously many times before the Republic finally shipped too much dirty water and sank. Aristocratic rivalry placed armies in private hands and dictatorships ceased to be a constitutional office and became the route to absolute personal power. But even when the Republic fell, the machinery of the state and the Empire itself continued.

The Romans themselves saw Julius Caesar's dictatorship and his succession by Augustus, his nephew, not as the beginning of Imperial authority, but simply as a change in the leadership of the Empire from the whole Senate to a *Princeps* (first magistrate) with dictatorial powers for life.[23]

Power-hungry, and usually corrupt, aristocrats like Sulla, Pompey and Caesar, together with their clients, destroyed free political institutions, but the forms of the *respublica* (or government in public for the public benefit) continued as an essential part of legitimacy. Augustus Caesar established the Emperor's Empire and deliberately cultivated *grandeur* and a show of imperial magnificence, both to overawe and impress and provide some substitute for the vanished (long vanished, in fact) republican simplicities. His head appeared on the coinage, like

31

some Hellenic tyrant, Eastern monarch or god, but also the words *'respublica'* and *'libertas'*; and he refused, unlike some of his successors, to be given divine honours in his life-time. In many ways he was a genuinely transitional or ambiguous figure between the temporary *Dictator* who came to save the republic and the *Imperator* who destroyed the republic and even sought to perpetuate his family in absolute power. He kept up the form of being appointed as *'Princeps'* or first magistrate (of the Republic) by a cowed Senate – indeed a Senate happy, in the main, to follow anyone who could restore peace, law and order after the Civil Wars of Caesar and Pompey, and who could ensure that no second Gracchi could lead the people against them, nor Spartacus the slaves.

Succession is, however, the Achilles' heel of any system of personal power. The authority of Augustus rested in practical terms on his leadership of and trust by the army, and on his role as peacemaker. But many of his successors lacked either his advantages or abilities. During the so-called *Principate* the Emperors went through the form of being nominated as *Princeps* by the Senate, but in fact they chose their successors and tried to train and build them up to size during their lifetime. Mostly they chose from their own families, but often used adoption as a device to pass-over a weak son for a tough nephew. When a successor was chosen from outside the genetic family, he was adopted into the legal family. But when Republican myths grew hollow and imperial ability slight, other bases for authority had to be found. An imperial cult was encouraged: the dead, even some of the living, emperors were worshipped as gods, who would then protect their descendants. Such imported oriental or late-Hellenistic ideas were greeted by ribald, but largely private, derision by the old Roman aristocracy: they may have had some influence on the people, but they served to alienate the educated classes from the state.[24] It was said that to the Roman people all religions were equally true, to the philosophers equally false, and to the magistrates equally useful.

A run of emperors of exceptional incompetence, cruelty and depravity put the selection for a time into the hands of the Palace or Praetorian Guard – when the famous auctioning of the office of Emperor occurred, a period which reached its climax in the 'year of the Four Emperors' when four rival armies fought for

32

their candidates. The one who survived this blood-bath, Vespasian, was able to curb the army, restore ordinary legality and carry through many reforms. He had himself recognised by the Senate to be absolute ruler in law as well as fact. He developed the idea that the successor should be chosen as the best man for the job, irrespective of birth or any real Senatorial concurrence. The forms of adoption were gone through and for a while the theory of the choice of the best man worked well, and the old doctrines of popular consultation were now no longer an assertion of rights but simply a reminder of ultimate political realities: Emperors had to convince the people that they were fit for the job and were, broadly speaking, governing with the people's interests in mind – otherwise authority crumbled. Four Emperors in succession. Trajan, Hadrian, Antonius Pius and Marcus Aurelius, 'maintained for more than eighty years a level of efficiency, devotion and commonsense which, except for a few periods both brief and rare, had not been known since the days of Augustus'.[25] But Aurelius, the philosopher emperor, chose his son, and Commodus proved to be a psychopathic wild-beast. He was murdered and the throne seized by a soldier, from which time on there was no more pretence at *Principate* but only the *Dominate* : autocracy without principles and based upon military force. There was light and there was shade. Christianity was first persecuted for its refusal to give any place to any other gods, particularly those of state cults for living Caesars; and then it was itself adopted as the state religion in a desperate attempt to find some new principles of unity. But regimes so personal and unstable could not grapple with the formidable economic problems of monopolies, famine and inflation, nor could they mobilise the old civic spirit to fill the legions with loyal and skilled men as vast tribal wanderings of barbarians began to press on the northern and north-eastern frontiers. When the Goths sacked Rome, the Empire had already fallen.

But in the early days of the *Principate* the military system was perfected and the legal system further developed. Even in the worst days of the *Dominate* in Rome itself, taxes continued to be gathered, aqueducts built and justice given freely and reasonably quickly and honestly in the Provinces. The legal and administrative system showed an astonishing, if never complete, independence from the folly and destructiveness of the Emperor's court.

The growth of a field of private law continued, a body of codified maxims, derived from a basic rational principle and to be applied to specific instances. Two great maxims ran through all the law : 'So use your property as to injure no one else' and 'Render to each his own'. At the moments of cruellest abuse of power, the lawyers and the philosophers still discussed how the *ius gentium*, the observed regularities of law in the numerous different nations in the Empire, and the *ius naturale*, law as it could be deduced from philosophical right reason, were to be reconciled and brought closer together, and both used as a critique of the *ius civile* – the actual laws of the city of Rome.[26] To the political fact of Empire was added a stoic philosophy which ignored the cultural differences of the city-states, which to the Greek had been life and freedom itself, and which tried to see reason in every man as something universal (even if that meant that some beings, apparently men, were not really men at all since they made no use of reason). Plutarch described the doctrines of the Stoics : 'Men should not live their lives in so many civic republics . . . they should reckon all as their fellow-citizens.'[27] Some of the ideals of universal justice survived the brutalities of Imperial power.

6. ORIENTAL DESPOTISM

The Roman Empire never in fact knew total power. Power was limited by the inability to control the economy, by inefficiency, by instability, by corruption, by tradition and most of all by lack of a motive to attempt the transformation of society – such as ideologies have given to some modern states. Systems of government were often imposed on systems of society with astonishingly little systematic integration, leading lives of their own, the societies readily outliving states. 'Kings may come and Kings may go, but we go on forever', said the peasantry. Marxists and liberals today both see total power as a unique product of the modern world somehow related to science, technology, industrialism, comprehensive ideologies and, some say, secularisation : their 'necessary logic' or their wilful abuse.

But it is believed by some that there was total power in the ancient world even before the Industrial and the French Revolutions created the conditions for totalitarianism. When knowledge of the civilisations of the Near East, India and China grew in Europe during the sixteenth to eighteenth centuries, some scholars, like Montesquieu in his *Spirit of the Laws* and Ferguson, the teacher of Adam Smith, thought that they had discovered a form of government, which they called 'oriental despotism', which stepped right outside the hitherto acceptable Aristotelian categories. Marx himself admitted 'Asiatic production', based on massive irrigation projects controlled by a highly centralised bureaucratic state, as an independent category: an exception to his otherwise simple progression from primitive society to feudal, from feudal to capitalist and from

35

capitalist to communist – all representing an ascending order of the concentration of power.[28] Engels was ambivalent towards the concept, Lenin wriggled around it and Stalin, seeing it as a possible reflection on Russia, cut the Gordian knot of theory by simply removing references to Asiatic production from the official editions of Marx. Recently the concept has been revived in a book that seems written for the ages, Karl Wittfogel's *Oriental Despotism*.[29]

Wittfogel, like Montesquieu before him, does not argue that massive irrigation by itself creates despotism. The waterworks of the Netherlands, of the Po Plain and of Venice all flourished under republics or far more traditional and limited autocracies and had a strongly defined private ownership of property. There are other motives, as we have seen, for imperial government; but the conditions of agriculture and population which called forth vast projects of hydraulic engineering furnish the opportunity for uniquely strong forms of despotism to arise. They were clearly unlike anything known in the autocracies of Europe – though with some tendencies that way in the later Roman Empire, in Byzantium and in Moorish Spain. Certainly even in those empires which spread over very mixed areas, not all of them dependent on centrally controlled hydraulic engineering, the response of the state to the needs of the irrigation projects tended to override everything else, and to necessitate a degree of positive mobilisation of the population for public works unknown until the twentieth century. The Babylonian and Assyrian Empires, China during the periods of unification, the great empires of India, the Arab Caliphate, Ottoman Turkey, the Inca Empire, and the federation of Aztec Mexico, all exhibit most or many of the features of oriental despotism. Egypt, Babylonia and Persia appear to be almost pure cases.

Certainly oriental despotism was stronger and more pervasive than either modern European autocracy of the sixteenth- to nineteenth-century kind or Roman power at most periods. Vast numbers of people were controlled and exploited by a few and on a scale far greater and with bureaucratic institutions far more elaborate than under the personal tyrannies of city-states. But it is doubtful if it was 'total' in a twentieth-century sense. The regimes had no object beyond territorial expansion (sometimes

36

not even that in their most stable periods) and survival: they neither sought nor needed the kind of power required to effect revolutionary changes or to transform societies. There was general conscription, but only for very specific purposes – canal building and maintenance – compared to modern industrial mobilisation, and then for limited periods only: for if the peasants did not return to their villages to reap and sow, the society would starve. In practice the peasantry had a tighter hold on land and personal property than did the bureaucracy: individually they were without legal rights and utterly helpless against abuse of authority, but collectively they had to be or simply were left a substantial degree of automony. And there were some possibilities of opposition, particularly in the cities and by the sons of kings. Total power, perhaps, but then power only in the important but limited sense of the terrible unchallengeability and unaccountability of authority, but not power in the sense of the ability to bring about great social changes – as self-styled 'totalitarian' regimes have attempted in the twentieth century. Except occasionally for religious proselytism, they had no such motives: they were regimes whose legitimacy depended on maintaining the *status quo*, not high rates of change or development. But 'oriental' despotism was a distinctive form of government, almost wholly untouched by the Greek tradition of politics and speculation about political justice, and *some* of whose features occur in contemporary Russian and Chinese government and stem from roots quite outside European conditions and the world-changing ideas that have sprung from them.[30]

7. FEUDAL GOVERNMENT

The usual fate of both the vast universal empires and the more specific systems of oriental despotism was to fall apart, though perhaps only after many centuries, through foreign invasion or by provincial governors or royal princes setting up as kings on their own. Such highly systematised and centralised governments could never devolve power without breaking up the whole structure; they could only splinter or break up, and sometimes vanish under the desert when central management of the canals and aqueducts broke down. They never evolved like the former Roman lands of the West into highly pluralistic and locally based power-system of feudalism, except perhaps in Japan. Feudalism was a distinct growth, certainly in Europe, a fusion of primitive Germanic government with Roman administrative, legal and religious (meaning by then Christian) remains.

Feudalism was a distinct growth, certainly in Europe, a fusion ing property in cattle, but later in land, and from which '*fief*' derives.[31] Such property was personal, in the sense of possession, but also communal in that it must be used for the common benefit. A strong sense of ownership in land and things arose compared to that of the ruling class in the Eastern empires, but weak and limited by traditional and customary obligations when compared to modern capitalism. Ownership was always limited by the traditional rights of others and by personal duties towards tenants: even serfs, unlike slaves, had some minimal feudal rights. Thus feudalism describes a system of limited and conditional loyalty and service, not of unconditional subservience; a system of vassalage, not of bureaucracy, and of land-ownership in a *fief*, that is to say in return for services to a superior, but held personally and in a family nonetheless, not just by virtue of office. To kill a rebel, for example, was customary, but to confiscate his lands was felt to be abominable, and a threat to all. Such a system grew to dominance in medieval Europe and in medieval Japan – that is to say right up to the end of the Tokugawa period in 1867 when a 'restoration' of imperial and central authority began an incredibly radical, swift and state-controlled policy of westernisation. Feudalism occurred so rarely elsewhere that it can be considered specific to these societies.[32]

R. S. Rattray, the anthropologist, had suggested that feudalism existed in the great nineteenth-century Ashanti kingdom now part of modern Ghana.[33] The Asantehene, or king, was surrounded by officials who held their stools or offices by family right, and the Amenhene, or sub-chiefs, held their annual *odwira* (oath-taking) and loyalty-pledging ceremonies for *their* men, but only after they had attended the king's *odwira*. It seemed all very feudal. But recent research has shown that this was only ever true for the relatively small circle of the 'true Ashanti' chiefs. The chiefs of the protected or conquered tribal governments had royal officials sitting alongside them with complete powers of veto, and throughout the nineteenth century this system for the vassal states was increasingly adopted even in the Akan heart-land. The Ashantis gained the power to appoint their own nominees to the other offices, a system which reverted to 'something like feudalism' only *after* the military defeat of the Ashantis by the British in the 1890s and the deliberate decentralisation that followed.[34]

In Europe, the Germanic systems of primitive government had only given the chief a limited dominance, sometimes even an elective position : the chieftain or king ranked first, but first among equals, at least there was a rough equality in these warrior bands who later grew into an aristocracy. The Germanic chieftain became the knight and the Roman lawyer became the priest. The European system of feudalism had astonishing similarities with the Tokugawa nobility or Samurai in Japan, their system of land-ownership, the relationships with the emperor and peasantry, and their *bushido* cult or ethic of 'honour' which, in one sense, bound them to their feudal superiors but in another limited those superiors to do nothing inconsistent with their liegeman's honour.

Feudalism took on many different local forms, even within one kingdom; but generally its main characteristics were something like this: (i) hierarchical relationships of lord and vassal, based on mutual service; these override any relationships to the king, emperor or even the kingdom: (ii) a highly personal form of government in which power was divided between many persons, and was most effective at a local level, less so centrally; (iii) the nobility administer things directly with very little functional differentiation of offices, only geographical – thus there is no ruling bureaucracy; (iv) a system of land-owning consisting in the granting or recognition of a *fief* (not an absolute right) in return for specified services and promised loyalty; (v) the recognised existence of private armies, together with a code of honour in which family attachments figure largely ('What's honour?', gibes Falstaff – a very bourgeois, anti-feudal figure – 'can it mend a wound?'); and (vi) the local lords have their own courts and judge their own cases among or against the peasants; but there are also royal courts (often church courts too) with a different but an overlapping jurisdiction – thus high and low justice.[35]

The overlap and conflict of jurisdictions made feudalism an increasingly legalised system – certainly a system that bred lawyers. Ideas of Roman law were revived and blended with the common or traditional law. All thinking men believed beyond doubt that each kingdom had a constitution, which was the whole body of its customs and that the exercising of authority was bound by law in two other ways: by God's law and by natural law (or right reason). This was taken for granted: argument prevailed 'only' on, for instance, who was to interpret God's law. Was it to be the Church as the institution of priesthood or the Church as the congregation of all Christians – which then included emperors and kings – but also barons and knights? And did the king, particularly the German Emperor, have some special sacred power? No one doubted that there were some things which must be rendered to God but also some to Caesar, just as some things were due to the king and some to the local lord – there was a basic dualism in both Christianity and feudalism: but no one could say with certainty, in either case, where the line should be drawn. All these questions were canvassed, sometimes with fire and sword. There was no ultimate way of enforcing these

40

delimitations but by violence, yet the sheer belief in a 'natural law' was important as a day-to-day restraint.

It was commonly held that the king could not *make* new laws, he could only declare what the 'good old laws' were, and then only after consulting his peers. The monarch in the feudal kingdom of England was, according to all the best authorities, both *politicum et regale*, political and absolute: political in that he had to consult before declaring the (everlasting) law, but absolute in power to enforce that law, to keep the peace and to defend the realm. It grew more and more a *political* system; effective power depended on persuasion and armed followers whom you could not wholly count upon.[36]

Estates or Parliaments were, in Christendom, typical feudal devices, gradually evolving from periodic 'Great Councils' of all leading men when the kings could no longer pay for government from their own estates and needed to raise taxation, which could only in fact be collected by the local magnates: hence *parles-mentium*, palaver or consultation before action. The English parliament is often mistakenly called 'the mother of parliaments' (it might be better to call it the Great Survivor of parliaments). The Icelandic *Althing* has, for instance, a longer continuous history as a representative assembly. Parliaments were the rule rather than the exception in the polities of feudal Europe. Early parliaments were judicial bodies rather than legislative, but at all times they were political: they arose to conciliate differences, or to obtain common action among diverse interests.[37] They emerged clearly towards the end of the twelfth century in the kingdom of León in Spain; in the thirteenth century they were flourishing in Catalonia, Sicily, Languedoc, Castille, Portugal, the *Reichstag* in the German Empire, Aragon, Navarre, Bohemia, Brandenburg, Austria, Valencia, Piedmont, England and Ireland; and by the fourteenth century in Sweden, Denmark, Norway and Poland.[38] Most disappeared in the sixteenth century, more at the time of the French Revolution and the autocratic reaction; only a handful survived.

In the fourteenth and fifteenth centuries they were more often divided into three houses or chambers, rather than two: usually of the nobles, the clergy and representatives of the towns. As the king and the pope, with uneasy division of powers, were felt to represent divine order, so the parliaments were felt to

41

represent the essential constituents of a natural social order – the three estates. The clerical, the military and the merchant classes were the politically effective classes, the old Roman republican concept of *'populus'* meant little in the medieval world, except in a few Italian and German self-governing or partly self-governing cities. Only in Sweden, Denmark, Norway and the Tyrol were peasants specifically represented. Peasantry have usually been an inert political force compared to the inhabitants of cities, as the very word 'citizen' suggests. But within and between the three estates there was active politics. It is the crudest misunderstanding to think of medieval kingship as in any way analogous to despotism.[39] Feudalism was a highly de-centralised social and political system, more often lacking in effective central power for the common good than enjoying too much power over the liberties of the localities. Knowing neither the concept of 'state' nor that of 'nation', and without an established bureaucracy, the medieval monarch was in constant need of the support of the influence of the Church, the coercion of the sword or the power of the purse – that is, from one or other of the three estates.

Thus here was a society with highly intellectualised ideas of religion, law and peace, but a society more and more in war and turmoil due to the lack of central power and the plentitude of local arms. Consider the richness of dress and also the fantastic beauty and elaboration of the cathedrals, but contrast them with the grim and entirely functional architecture of the castles. The great nobility could have lived more comfortably had they dared. But each man retired into the strength of his own stronghold : he went to court as little as possible compatible with suspicion of rebellion. 'Why comes young Harry Percy not to court?' The king, like his judges, was largely peripatetic, visiting and watching, restless, gregarious yet fearful. But tyranny and despotism were rare or unknown: 'liberties' were many, possibly too many, for men's minds began to turn towards strengthening the king in the hope of avoiding the anarchy of private wars.

8. THE EARLY MODERN STATE

'The modern state is a European, or more exactly, Western European, creation', Heinz Lubatz has written.[40] The modern state is, above all else, a sovereign state: it seeks to be the sole authority and the only effective power within a given territory, and seeks also to preserve the independence of that territory. In the early modern period this did not necessarily imply even in theory, certainly never in fact, an unlimited or total domination: the state was held to be predominant, but not omnipotent; unchallengeable, but not omnicompetent. It sought to preserve peace and order, not to change society drastically (however much and however rapidly societies were, in fact, changing); it is only in the later modern period, certainly not earlier than the nineteenth century, that men came to believe that states could and should transform society.

Unlike Venus Aphrodite, nothing is born fully formed from the sea-foam. Many medieval monarchs had striven consciously, with varying degrees of limited success, to centralise justice and administration in their own hands, to appeal to the 'people', the peasantry, the yeomanry or the cities above the heads of their feudal superiors; and, above all, to reduce the size of private armies and to level, limit or license the castles owned by their 'proud vassals', whom they would rather treat as subjects. Internal war was not suddenly seen as a problem at the end of the fifteenth century, nor did it vanish with the growth of the 'new monarchies', such as those of Charles V, Francis I or Henry VIII – as shown by the French Wars of Religion in the sixteenth century, the English Civil War and, above all, the

43

Thirty Years War in Germany in the seventeenth century.

But these political moves by monarchs seeking to impose a benovolent autocracy were strengthened during the fifteenth and sixteenth centuries by great forces of social change.[41] These forces were largely independent of anything but the most marginal control by either the old feudal monarchs or the new Renaissance Princes; yet they both sapped feudalism and gave governments new capabilities. The declining respect for the Church and the rise of Protestantism both damaged the moral restraints implicit in feudal divisions of power and strengthened the authority of princes: both the old Church and the new churches needed pious and armed protectors as never before, now no longer against the Arabs, the Mongols and the Turks (who all in turn had nearly conquered Christendom), but against their fellow Christians. Capitalism and the growth of a money market had already turned many vassal-services into cash payments and had led merchants and bankers into the councils and friendship of kings; and with the new Protestant attitude to wealth and the decay of Catholic restraints on usury and money-lending, capital became available: the king could provide the conditions of peace and justice necessary for trade and, in so far as he succeeded, his power and stability made him the most credit-worthy. All over continental Europe in the sixteenth century Estates and Parliaments met for the last time, as monarchs found sources of wealth that were independent of bargaining with their too-powerful subjects.

Military technology also played a role in the decay of feudalism and the centralisation of power. Cannons had sacred texts on their barrels and traditional emblems, but they had to be cast in elaborate workshops easy for the crown to take over or control. Everywhere kings attempted, with varying degrees of success, to gain a monopoly of *effective* arms. The nobility were generally allowed, for the first time, to carry personal arms in their sovereign's presence, for what were swords and rapiers compared to arquebus and cannon? Cardinal Richelieu strove to put down duelling; Cardinal Mazarin saw no reason why the aristocracy should not kill themselves off so cheaply. But private armies were put down and the wearing of livery limited to household servants.

Princes also strove to gain a monopoly of skilled counsel from those advisers loyal only to themselves or, as the advisers began to think, servants of 'the State' – not of the Church or of a noble house. Thus 'new men', 'upstarts', 'Jacks in office' and *parvenus* – or scholars and humanists, in other words, began to come close to the seats of power. They usually brought skill and order and some continuity into state business.[42] The commissariat with inventoried lists and the archive arranged by administrative function, not by area, become the inner fact and symbol of this new type of government – not such a bureaucratic government in Europe as in China, still a highly personal government, perhaps more personal and capricious than ever. But the prince now had the capability of offices and bureaucracy behind him, not just the aura of office. The new men were mostly lawyers from the universities. New colleges and universities were founded under royal or princely patronage, no longer directly or exclusively under Church control, specifically to ensure the supply of these men and, in varying degrees, to control their education.

These men either brought with them new ideas or they skilfully rationalised tendencies already afoot. The idea of 'the state' itself is a Renaissance invention or revival. 'The word "state" crystallised in the sixteenth and seventeenth centuries', wrote Carl Joachim Friedrich, 'because secular rulers who wanted to achieve absolute power needed a symbol that they could set against the Church, something that would be awe-inspiring and clothed with an abstract corporate halo.'[43]

Feudal privileges were suppressed 'in the name of the state'. This new phrase was both a threat and a guarantee : no man had rights against the state, but the state existed to preserve national independence, internal peace, law and order. This phrase was sufficient to establish the authenticity of a command from the king, by seal, ring, or signature – it was unnecessary and seditious to question the reason. Machiavelli argued that when the safety of the state was threatened, 'no consideration of good or evil, mercy or cruelty' should stand in the way of its resolute preservation. He did not mean anything as mad or Nietzschean as that good and evil were meaningless, but simply – as his beloved Ancient Romans would have understood – that without the state no forms of civilised life is possible.[44]

The doctrine of sovereignty was made explicit for the first time by Jean Bodin in the midst of the French Wars of Religion. He,

45

too, was a humanist, a member of the party of Michel L'Hôpital, nicknamed '*Les Politiques*', who argued for religious toleration as a political necessity. The king must be 'sovereign', above all human laws and restraint, although Bodin was still medieval enough to say that the king was bound by God's laws and the natural law; but God would settle all accounts, it was not for barons or parliaments to presume to sit in armed judgement.[45]

The predominance of the secular was asserted, even revelled in, but it did not abolish faith, it simply established a new and more clear-cut boundary; nor must one exaggerate the rationality of the new statecraft and philosophy of the state. The doctrine of reason of state (*raison d'État* or *staatsräson*, as vernacular replaced latinity) held that there were some things which ordinary subjects should never question, indeed could never even know. The idea emerged of the '*arcana imperii*', or 'mysteries' of power (as in medieval craft-guild mysteries): a prince needed reason and technical knowledge as never before, but this would be useless without strong *will*, the *libido dominandi*, and some inborn or God-given flair for government – almost a great artist's mixture of technique and inspiration.[46] So authority became a blend of both power and majesty, and majesty was expressed in the grandeur of the new palaces: built to impress the magnificence of the monarch upon, and his almost god-like distance from his subjects, no longer the grim defensive castle. Even the German princes of even the smallest principalities built, upon the backs of their subjects, huge palaces whose every architectural feature strove for the illusion of absolute power.[47]

46

9. THE MODERN NATION STATE

So 'the state', strictly speaking, is a unique form of government unknown in Europe before the fifteenth and sixteenth centuries, and reaching its full development in the seventeenth century. It is this form of state which Max Weber's famous definition – the monopolist of the legitimate means of violence – alone fits.[48] As the concept developed, it became associated with an attendant philosophy – that of sovereignty, and an attendant form of society – that of a nation. From a world that had known such varying and sometimes coexisting forms of government as would-be universal empires, city-states, the great hybrid of Rome, despotism and feudalism, there eventually emerged with the age of discovery and the brief period of European global imperialism, a world entirely constituted of nation states all claiming sovereignty.

It was Thomas Hobbes, rather than Jean Bodin, who first developed an entirely consistent and religiously uninhibited theory of sovereignty – in his book *Leviathan*. It was written, during the English Civil War, in order to teach men, he said, the grim consequences of 'the false opinion that power can be divided'. Law, he taught, is nothing but the command of someone with the power to enforce it: 'covenants without the sword are vain'; and 'private judgements of right and wrong' destroy the whole basis of authority and would plunge society into what would, just like the states among themselves, be anarchy or 'a state of nature', the *bellum omnes contra omnes* – the war of all against all. But, in fact, Hobbes' masterly analysis of the alternatives before government and society contains profound and

47

deliberate ambiguity.[49] The grounds on which the state should be obeyed derive from two 'laws of nature' or self-evidently true maxims : to seek peace and to preserve one's individual life. While the state can do this, there is no rational questioning of its authority; but once it ceases to be able to, it ceases to exist and obligation should be given to whoever else can. If Shakespeare has in him a bit of the same spirit as Hobbes, then the hero of Bosworth Field is not Harry Tudor, but the politic Stanley who sits waiting to see which way the wind is blowing before he renders the probable result certain. In other words, the theory of sovereignty if pressed that far removes the last vestige of primitive, personal and feudal loyalty – as Hobbes intended : a man is a fool who fights for a lost cause, and is *only* 'dishonourable', he says, not a traitor, if he runs away in battle if his life is in danger. Unless the state is accepted as an 'end in itself' (which to Hobbes would have been unrealistic nonsense), its justification depends on a purely utilitarian service to individuals. *Leviathan* can point forward either to benevolent despotism and the autocracy of the Enlightenment, or to a full nineteenth-century individualism. 'Hobbes', said Bentham, 'was the father of us all'.[50]

In fact Hobbes cared profoundly, almost to a fault, for a new thing called 'the individual', man stripped of all religious or group identity. Until the French Revolution, the sovereign state lacked any motive to threaten to change individuals, so long as they kept quiet. Hobbes's good Monarch would not be always stirring things up, but quietly monopolising power and letting individuals carry on with their trade, commerce and learning. Charles II, trying to govern without parliaments but with great restraint and prudence, is a better picture of what Leviathan would have been than, say, Tsar Peter or Napoleon.

Nor did sovereignty necessarily imply one man. In England as in the French, Spanish and Habsburg states, the royal advisers of Henry VIII had been tempted, like the king himself, to suppress parliament and to assert the maxim of the late Roman law over the common law : '*Quod principi placuit, leges habet vigorem*' (what pleases the prince has the force of law). Few nations avoided autocracy before the French Revolution – England was able to blend the autocratic and the republican traditions. An example from Tudor politics will show how the

48

conscious will to autocracy could temper itself with political prudence in such a way that possibilities of both constitutional and autocratic government were left open and ambiguous.

A former Chancellor of England, Stephen Gardiner, is defending, from prison, his conduct in the reign of Henry VIII:

> The Lord Cromwell had once put into the King our late sovereign lord's head to have his will and pleasure regarded as a law: for that, he said, was to be a very king. And thereupon I was called for at Hampton Court, . . . 'Answer the king here', quoth he, 'but speak plainly and directly and shrink not, man! Is not that that pleaseth the king, a law? Have you not there in the Civil [Roman] Law', quoth he, ' *"quod principi placuit"* and so forth, I have somewhat forgotten it now.' I stood still and wondered in my mind to what conclusion this should tend. The King saw me musing and with earnest gentleness said, 'Answer him, whether it be so or no.' I . . . told him that I had read indeed of kings that had their will always received for a law; but, I told him, by the form of his reign, to make the laws his will was more sure and quiet. 'And by thy form of government you are established', quoth I, 'and it is agreeable with the nature of your people. If you begin a new manner of policy, how it will frame, no man can tell; and how this frameth, ye can tell; and I would never advise your Grace to leave a certain for an uncertain.' The King turned his back and left the matter after.[51]

The real Machiavellian meets the pseudo-Machiavellian. The Tudor monarchs had more power governing through Parliament than if they had tried, as their successors were to try so unsuccessfully, governing without it. The king, with some ups and downs, revelled in the popularity he could draw from Parliament and the political strength that went with it, particularly from the House of Commons. The English lawyers proclaimed that the King's power was 'never so great as when he sat in Parliament'. The power of the Crown (the very concept 'State' seemed strange in England) later came into conflict with the old feudal pretensions of Parliament.[52] The 1630s and the 1680s proved that kings could not rule without parliaments, just as the 1650s had proved that parliaments could not govern by them-

49

selves. The reality which emerged between 1688 and 1780 was that the Crown, or the King's Ministers, could only rule through Parliament: by the eighteenth century the theory stood on its head and the 'sovereignty of Parliament' could be asserted.

Only the English colonists in America went so far as to challenge sovereignty itself, and to seek for a form of government subject to natural law. They showed the survival, as did John Locke's writings, of basically medieval ideas of natural and divine restraints upon governments.[53] The American example was formidable. Throughout the nineteenth century men living in autocracies demanded to be given or to be allowed to make a constitution; or elsewhere, as in the old republics of Switzerland and the Netherlands, they sought for new and better ones. They differed from the English seventeenth-century parliament men in that these new radicals now thought that they were making new institutions, not demanding the return of old ones. The American Constitution was almost perfectly poised between tradition and aspiration. But even in the Philadelphian Constitution of 1787, harsh reality forced the office of President to be also that of commander-in-chief, and implied provisions for emergency powers were found when needed. 'Tell him to send some one round to talk to me about it after the war', said Lincoln when the Chief Justice at the beginning of the Civil War declared his seizure of the new telegraphs unconstitutional. It is doubtful, in fact, if constitutional restraints can ever be as decisive as people once believed – compared, say, to the political traditions of a country and its actual social divisions of power.

The absence of a formal constitution does not necessarily point to autocracy, only to the presence of or the need for a political tradition. There must be 'autocratic' or 'authoritarian' elements in any form of government that is to survive; the question is not whether these tendencies exist, but how are they controlled? How do they fit into the whole political culture? Some governments suffer opposition – a very few encourage it; some profess to believe that 'in the circumstances' it (always) endangers the safety of the state, so cannot be tolerated; and others, the truly autocratic, hate it on principle – but even so, they are usually limited by prudence.

The only motive to see the state as an end in itself was

50

furnished by the growth of national sentiment and nationalism. National sentiment began to be important in some of the new states of the early modern period: when kings sought popularity among 'their people', that is, sought to suborn the vassals of their own vassals; then they would not appeal to dynastic loyalty, but to national loyalty – the 'King of the French' not just 'the King of France'. But this was a long way from modern nationalism: a state might contain several national groups, and the great dynasties themselves fished in many ethnically, religiously and linguistically muddied waters; and the claim that the state belonged to its people had to be resisted.

Modern nationalism is either democratically based or it involves an autocracy in stirring up and managing 'the people', whereas the older dynastic autocracies preferred to let sleeping dogs lie.[54] Patriotism could easily get out of hand and end up in claims that 'This land is my land' simply because I live and work in it. Nationalism as a principle of government is no older than the French Revolution, though historians will dispute for ever whether it came first from the Jacobin armies, or from the resistance to Napoleon in Europe. It is the belief that the only just and possible unit of rule is a territory coterminous with a nation.[55] Rulers, bureaucrats and subjects must be of one nation; each nation must form a state and each state should contain no more than one nation. It has often been a democratic doctrine, but nearly always an illiberal one. Taken together, as Napoleon was able to do for purposes of war, the slogan and the reality of 'the nation' and 'the people' constituted an almost unique strength. The inhabitants of France, being fired with patriotic ardour, could be generally rather than selectively trusted with arms and could be conscripted without danger to the rulers. The *levée en masse*, the introduction to Europe (or its re-invention) of this typical institution of despotism, was only possible in a nationalistic context. Some nation states allowed full political liberty to their own full nationals, and merely discriminated against minorities; some allowed not even such limited freedom.

The state, as Machiavelli had seen in his great *Discourses*, could equally well take, mostly according to circumstances, somewhat according to will and skill, a republican or an autocratic form; and this is as true for the nation state as for the few multinational states.

51

10. MODERN AUTOCRACY

As I will show more fully in Part Two, the Model, I think there are basically three broad forms of contemporary government: autocracies, republics and totalitarian regimes. Only the third has any great claim to be distinctly modern and it is the only form now, with the collapse of the colonial empires, which imperial authority is ever likely to take. The basic features of autocratic government precede the industrial revolution. Industrialism creates huge problems as well as opportunities for government: many unique devices of government and even of representations are invented; literate populations pose unique problems of control and proper employment; and universal ideas of human rights both make opportunities for freedom greater and make tasks of repression more massive and grim. But despite a lot of rhetoric about new conditions demanding new institutions, examples of new institutions are either very small in scale (like *communes* or *kibbutzim*) or, as yet, trivial in impact (like the World Court and the United Nations Organisation). Old forms of government have been adapted and have proved remarkably resilient – with one possible exception.

Most governments in the modern world are still autocratic.[56] They may aspire to be 'new in all things', but military juntas or party elites behave depressingly like aristocratic or dynastic ruling groups. Occasionally they aspire to be 'totalitarian', but usually that too is just empty rhetoric. They have vast power that is unchallengeable, but the power is often pathetic if seen in terms of the ability to carry out premeditated intentions – particularly when the intentions are as vast and vague as

52

'modernisation', 'industrialisation' and 'national reconstruction'. Autocracy was the typical form of European government from the time of the Renaissance until its challenge by the French Revolution and eventual collapse in the First World War. If autocracy in the twentieth century seems to many an anachronism, working against so many modernising tendencies of the times, then this only shows how few modern (contemporary is better) states are, in fact, genuinely trying to modernise or are genuinely succeeding. Spain, Portugal, the Arab kingdoms and sheikdoms openly preserve traditional autocracy, and the autocracies of South-East Asia, South America and Africa, if trying to modernise, yet seem more prone to instability and internal violence. And the vast disparity of wealth between rich and poor societies tends to discredit the stable and relatively rich republican regimes, as if freedom for some is not the example to be extended but the condition for the suffering of many – as Marxists believe.

Autocracy I take to be the form of government which attempts to solve the basic problem of the adjustment of order to diversity by the enforcement of one of the diverse interests as the only ideology to be tolerated and sponsored. It does not attempt to get rid or to transform all other groups or classes in the state, it simply reduces them to subservience : it has no motive to get rid of them, compared to totalitarian regimes, and usually no power to do so either. Autocracy was and is often as frightening in its powerlessness and inefficiency as it was and is in its arbitrariness and unchallengeability. No one can rival the autocrat, but the autocrat can be hideously ineffectual.

They demand, but are usually cynical about, active enthusiasm from some, but not all. The rulers try to maintain a highly stratified caste or class society – although the shrewder autocrats recruit administrators outside their own group, just as the shrewder aristocracies skimmed off the cream of native ability. Napoleon is the archetypal shrewd autocrat with his creation of an 'aristocracy of merit' and 'the careers open to all talents'. The Government House has now replaced the Court or the Palace; and huge concrete office blocks have replaced the magnificent and awesome royal dwellings and the 'gilded cages' of the nobility; but their function is much the same.

The economy remains typically highly agrarian – cities seem to breed free men or true citizens or to compel extreme measures

53

of despotism; usually the traditional European autocrats were not able to control the cities as tightly as they controlled the countryside. Usually the actual agricultural system is basically that of subsistence peasant small-holdings, a commercial agriculture creates a powerful class of small capitalist middle-men; and also the gentry and the aristocracy rarely farm the land themselves – which explains the ultimate social and economic strength of the English gentry against the Crown, and the endemic weakness of the French aristocracy. Autocracies practise political censorship and destroy, with or without the law, open political opposition; but autocracies can at times be tolerant of dissent within the party or ruling class, so long as it is not made public. The religious basis of autocratic authority wanes, but it is replaced by doctrines which attribute almost superhuman qualities to the leader or leaders of the moment. Hence censorship is a general but a negative institution, not a positive and total propaganda; hence there are proclamations, but neither regular nor even remotely objective and believable news; and therefore rumour, gossip and anonymous satires and 'libels' flourish as institutions. The regime itself gets into difficulties through flatterers and lack of proper 'feed-back', hence much spying and the odd institutions of barbers and court jesters (which Hitler and Nkrumah, in their different ways, used just as much as a Renaissance monarch). The regime pictures itself as either 'above politics' (politics being seen as conspiracy against the state), or politics is to be strictly limited to within the walls of the Palace, the Court or the Party H.Q. In all the last three categories there is often an astonishing amount of free speculation, but only 'within these four palace walls' : nothing must get out that might shake the faith of the people or their belief that their rulers are, from their point of view, hopelessly omniscient and united. But stability of government in an autocracy is commonly purchased at the price of social and economic stagnation. Autocrats are strong in the business of oppression, but are usually weak in responding to sudden social or economic change. Usually they collapse from their own rigidity and incompetence, far more than by the efforts of the oppressed.

54

11. MODERN REPUBLICS

To call systems of government democratic can be extremely misleading. There is scarcely a regime in the modern world that does
not claim to be democratic.[57] The Russians and the Chinese are as
sure that they are democratic as are the Americans and Dutch.
Two quite different things can be meant by democracy: it can
simply mean 'popular power', as it meant in the Greek city-states
or in the Paris of the Revolution of 1789; or it can mean
individualism, liberty and toleration. Obviously many people
want both, and to some extent democracy as 'popular power
plus liberty' does, very roughly, describe the social and political
reality in the United States – which is particularly insistent on
calling itself 'democratic'. But it is perfectly possible, indeed common, for majorities to be highly intolerant – as when Tocqueville
and J. S. Mill spoke of the 'tyranny of the majority' and the
threat that democracy can pose to liberty. It is less common, but
possible, for minorities in power to be extremely tolerant:
Voltaire and the young Bentham pinned their hopes on 'En-
lightened Autocracy' rather than, with Rousseau, on popular
democracy.

Neither usage is inherently more correct than the other. But
there are advantages in using it in the Russian or the French
revolutionary way: simply to describe the reality in which all
governments after the time of the French and the industrial
revolutions, that is all governments involved in deliberate social
change or modernisation, depend upon the support of the masses
and upon being able to mobilise, or at least change the working
habits of the masses, in the way that no ancient or early modern

55

autocracy needed to do. They may carry this consent by fraud, propaganda and indoctrination, but carry it they must: they need the energy of the population, not just its passivity. 'The politics of the future', said Napoleon, 'will be the art of stirring the masses.' And he, unlike the Prussians and the Austrians, could trust his people with arms, so he could introduce mass conscription, whereas the traditional autocracies only dared conscript and recruit highly selectively.

In the sense that all modern or modernising governments are democratic, one can distinguish three broad types: the communist claim that democracy is 'the dictatorship of the proletariat' – no nonsense about liberty until the last remnants of bourgeois opposition have vanished; the nationalist claim that democracy is simply the fraternity or national communion of rulers and people being of one nation; and Anglo-American – or, some might say, in origins at least – the liberal-capitalist creation or enforcement of a purely individualistic approach to rights.[58]

Therefore the term 'republican' is preferable to 'democratic' when we want to make quite clear that it is liberty *and* popular power that we are discussing as the characteristic of some modern governments. Indeed, it helps us to see that 'popular power' is itself a relative term: England in the eighteenth century clearly had a free parliament and allowed public contest for office and debates over matters of state, long before a democratic franchise emerged. The American statesmen of 1787 nearly all saw, in traditional and correct classical terms, democracy as a necessary element in just government, but not the only one.

'Republican government' is then the form of government which attempts to solve the basic problem of the adjustment of order to diversity by conciliating different interests either by letting them share in the government or at least in the competitive and public choosing of the government or the assembly from which it is chosen. Positive demands are put upon the individual inhabitants of republics: that all can and some must participate in affairs of state, that is to say exercise 'citizenship'. Public and private life are distinguished, both in morality and law, and men can move freely from one to the other; but the thing simply does not work if some considerable number of men do not voluntarily take part in public affairs. Allegiance is demanded and given primarily on utilitarian and secular grounds; practical benefits

56

in the sweet here-and-now must be shown, not just promised in the sour by-and-by. There is typically a fairly stable political class enjoying social prestige by virtue of office, but a class penetrable to some significant extent by candidates from educational institutions designed to increase social mobility. The typical institution of government is an assembly, congress or parliament, but note that these rarely govern directly themselves, but are the medium *through* which governments and populations communicate and influence each other.

It is believed that information about government and political news should be broadcast and is, anyway, hard to stop; newspapers are freely available at all levels of society, and considerable objectivity grows up in official statistics and in studies of society. The first arguments for rights within autocratic government concentrated on claiming that laws or regulations should be known and general, that is not secret and uncertain or arbitrary and particular; in the first large republics men argued further that laws must be publicly debated before they could gain the force of law; and we are now hearing arguments to the effect that it is both right and efficient that the evidence on which a government decides to bring on new laws should also be made known. Political contestation is always tolerated, however condescendingly, often positively encouraged, but only by political means or within the limits of public order (although this itself is a relative term; different societies have different levels of tolerance to disorder); and a procedural rather than a substantive mentality emerges.

It is foolish to pretend that such a form of government is not obviously the best – in the sense of freedom and justice, of effectiveness and stability, and of providing conditions in which truths can be discovered and spoken. It is the best, but it is not always possible and, like any form of government, it demands a minimum of skill from its rulers – many can blunder almost as easily as a few; it also demands a minimum of understanding from its inhabitants of how things actually work; and it demands a minimum of effective compassion from the whole society towards other societies who may believe, rightly or wrongly, that freedom and prosperity for some are, at present, purchased at the price of subservience and poverty for others.

57

12. TOTALITARIAN GOVERNMENT

Autocracies, however arbitrary and cruel, had limited aims and were usually highly traditional. They rationalised tradition into philosophies of State, but their practical maxim of government was, almost invariably, *quieta non movere* – or 'let sleeping dogs lie'. They demanded passive obedience from all but never, outside the Court circles, positive and compulsory enthusiasm. Lickspittlery, sycophancy and toadying were, in those happy days, aristocratic arts, not ones the populace needed. Autocrats and even tyrants had limited aims, dynastic and personal. Usually they sought, in such dark times, simply to enjoy power. They were seldom, to speak mildly, dedicated to the reformation of mankind – though they often had strong views about the manners and morals of their subjects.

But in our century a few powerful regimes appear to have aimed at nothing less than the transformation of society and the regeneration of mankind. Mussolini first talked about 'a new totalitarian form of government' when his Fascists came to power in Italy in the 1920s. This was mainly claptrap: Italy remained an inefficient tyranny under the Fascists. They had remarkably little effect on Italian society, were mocked by the Nazis, and Mussolini was closer to the classical dictator than to the new style of leader which began to emerge among *both* the Nazis in Germany and the Communists in Russia and China.

Never have two regimes been less alike in their origins and their specific aims. The one claimed that *racial* factors explain everything and that the course of history is determined by the violent *struggles* of the racially superior to purify their lands from corrupting and corrosive elements, struggles fated to be be victorious

58

if the right *leader* emerged – the Nazi 'unholy trinity' of Race, Struggle and Leader. The other asserted Marx's theory that the economic factors are always finally decisive, that history is a process of revolutionary class struggle, and – the special theory to explain why the revolution in Russia did not lead to classlessness, freedom and equality overnight – that dictatorship by the proletariat (Lenin) or by the Communist Party (Stalin) must complete or speed-up the, of late, somewhat aborted processes of historical necessity. But there are also certain astonishing similarities between these two regimes when compared together against all previous forms of autocracy.[59] They were both concerned, like secular religions, to transform utterly all mankind according to the analysis, guidance and prophecies not just of doctrines, always somewhat limited in purpose, however passionately held, but of an 'ideology' aiming to explain everything.

In fact, total control, total explanation even, and certainly total transformation has proved impossible. No government, not even the Chinese Communists, still less Stalin's, far less Hitler's, has even come near to total control in the sense of transformation, although perhaps much nearer in the negative sense of wiping out opposition thoroughly, not just cutting off the heads but pulling up the roots also. But the attempt has led to a form of government quite unlike old tyranny and autocracy in its extent, and many of whose massive cruelties are only explicable in terms of the ideology, not in terms of political needs or sadistic caprice : the Nazi attempt to exterminate the Jews, Stalin's purges of the former bourgeoisie and the old peasantry, and the Chinese in like manner. The Nazis were defeated only by war;[60] the murderous paranoia of Stalin induced some kind of mutual tolerance in his successors – though almost entirely for their own benefit; and China, though torn with internal struggles, seems to grow more ideologically rigid, not less. Above all, totalitarianism, unlike old autocracy, depends upon mass support. It is, if a perversion of democracy, nonetheless a product of a democratic age : democracy as equality without freedom.

So totalitarian government is the attempt to solve the basic problem of the adjustment of order to diversity by creating a completely new society such that the conflict would no longer arise. It attempts to do this by means of the guidance and then the universal enforcement of a revolutionary ideology which

59

claims to be scientific, thus comprehensive and necessary, both for knowledge and allegiance. Of the inhabitants is demanded mass participation and compulsory enthusiasm – 'those who are not for us, are against us!'; and mistakes and inefficiency are branded as, and usually believed to be, sabotage. The official doctrine is claimed to be, technically and specifically, 'an ideology', a *Weltanschauung* or comprehensive world view, but revolutionary as well, to explain, control and predict everything important in society (in fact, there have only been two ideologies: that of race and that of economics – as in *Mein Kampf* and *Das Kapital*). They aspire to an egalitarian classlessness, racial or mass brotherhood, but in fact create a new class structure defined by bureaucratic function and political loyalty; and the 'take-off point' has been the shattering of traditional class barriers by war and mass-unemployment, rendering masses available for mobilisation by a determined and supposedly far-sighted elite.

The typical institution of government is a single party; and a single party that is a single party because it has deliberately destroyed all its rivals and opponents. Compared to older forms of autocracy or imperial authority, totalitarianism has greater powers of self-renewal and has clear methods and conventions for settling the succession. The economy is presented as a completely and rationally planned economy, but this, in fact, has never yet proved to be the case; planning in totalitarian regimes arose in practice from wartime conditions, the rejection for the 'duration of the crisis' of 'mere economic criteria'. And now the sense of crisis is perpetuated by belief in the need for *rapid* industrialisation (and rapidity is assumed to be essential at whatever the cost).

Attitudes to the diffusion of information are of the utmost importance in totalitarian regimes: the means of mass communication are rigorously controlled, and there is a compulsory market for them. The negative censorship of autocracy becomes a positive propaganda; but, as in autocracy, there is a terrible compulsion by the bureaucracy to tell the rulers what they want to hear, so an extreme unreliability of official statistics results, even for the inner-circle; and hence no reliable knowledge of either domestic or world opinion despite the *vast* numbers of people employed in the intelligence apparatus.

60

13. THE FUTURE OF GOVERNMENT

Having been so sweeping about the past, let us at least mention the most common theories about the future. Enough has been said to show that many of the things in government, good and bad, that we think of as distinctively modern have, in fact, a long and relevant history. But what is distinctively modern are rapid rates of change. Industrialisation as such has had less effect on both forms and aims of government than the general modern idea that change can be deliberately pursued for the better. All sorts of changes, however, are taking place in all sorts of directions at once, some contradictory, some irrelevant to each other but compatible, few without advocates, but none working out quite as their supporters intend.

Some of the distinctly modern theories about the main directions of change as they affect government are worth considering, however briefly.

1. That there will be government by scientists and technologists – as prophesied by Saint-Simon, George Bernard Shaw and H. G. Wells among them. But to what ends? Only very abstract answers like 'reason' can be given. 'Science' cannot define goals, nor even priorities among the multiplicity of goals, but only possibilities and means towards ends.[61]

2. That capitalism will collapse and that there will be revolutionary transformation of society such that a classless and strifeless society will follow. But capitalism has proved both more resilient and more capable of dilution than was expected, and socialism more ambiguous. There have only been three or four genuine examples of spontaneous revolutions in this century:

61

Russia (in February 1917), Mexico, Hungary (in 1956), China and possibly Cuba; but none of them have involved any total transformation of society, nor worked out as expected, nor served as models readily transplantable elsewhere.[62]

3. That 'the inevitability of gradualness' will lead to an evolutionary revolution in democratic societies (as the Webbs and John Dewey argued, in different ways). Perhaps in the long run this may be so, but in rapidly expanding societies, autocracy plainly has a role – as one-party states are typical in the Third World. But political freedom, while not ensuring progress, does seem to have positive advantages in stimulating, or at least not hindering, invention and hence the adaptability of societies. The old Social Democratic theorists were probably right : planning and freedom are not incompatible, but in the long run are functional requisites of each other.[63]

4. That we are heading for decay and catastrophe : men are becoming more and more uniform and dehumanised, and hence ripe for exploitation by those whose technical powers are uninhibited by natural or traditional morality. This is broadly speaking the general view of the future found in contemporary science-fiction, and in George Orwell's great *1984*. But they all underestimate the resilience of human freedom; they all have free heroes, even though they, like Winston Smith, fail or are beaten. Thus they are imaginative warnings of what could happen, not of what is likely to happen, on the record of civilisation so far.[64]

5. That all societies are converging into bureaucratically planned or managerial societies due to the common conditions and needs of 'highly industrial civilisation'. (This was often put forward in the 1950s and early 1960s to counter the now absurd-sounding 'bi-polar' theory, that everything was moving towards either the U.S.A. or the U.S.S.R.) Perhaps a half-truth, but just like the first theory, managers do not define their own aims, or if they have to by default of proper control, they are as likely to come up with several different packets of priorities as are any other group of men.[65]

6. That the Third World or the new societies will create new forms of government and styles of politics based on community rather than on either individualism or party dictatorship. Originally this theory arose simply as a political counter to the

62

U.S./U.S.S.R. bi-polar hypothesis, but then came to be seen as a positive way of stating a community of long-term interest among countries assumed to be underdeveloped or, more clearly and simply, poor. But while poverty is a common problem, solutions may be various : the only long-term reasons for supposing that a fundamental identity exists between such poor countries are political more than economic or social. These political factors diminish as the old bi-polar pattern grows less and less plausible, since so many tails wag the big dogs. Russia and the United States learn to live with each other but China remains ambiguous. Actual governments in the Third World are predominantly military in character and highly unstable, showing few original features, except perhaps the stress on co-operation and participation in Tanzania, Yugoslavia and Cuba (all heavily 'guided' democracies). With those exceptions, revolution is less a factor than the Ancient Greek '*stasis*' – violent and continual changes of power leaving society untouched or unreformed. In the few states which actually attempt rapid industrialisation, an autocratic form of government rarely proves capable of mobilising the population sufficiently for the prolonged and consistent effort and sacrifices needed to modernise swiftly. (Even the single-party autocracy, as in much of Africa, proves unexpectedly weak in this; the party itself often turns out to be the personal following of some leader, not a movement linking masses and elites).[66]

7. That national states are rapidly becoming universal – again a half-truth, for while a sense of nationality solves many of the above problems, and does effectively link rulers and ruled, it does not by itself define a just form of government, particularly for national minorities; it still needs reconciling with personal liberty if invention and hence flexibility are not to suffer, and it usually arouses a revolution of economic expectations which cannot, in the short or middle period, be satisfied, except by excessive reliance on investment by the Great Powers.

8. That, on the contrary, the nations of the world are moving towards world government. There is a powerful belief that this *should* be so, but few signs that it will be so. World government would either imply universal disarmament, or a world monopoly of arms. Only the latter could enforce the former, and the latter is more likely to come through conquest than by general consent. But if world 'government' is unlikely, the political

institutions of the United Nations do have some restraining effect. The UNO will not grow towards a world government, but will become increasingly effective in publicising the risks of armed conflict and in policing and enforcing the terms of settlement.[67]

9. That government itself is so grossly oppressive and bureaucratic, in the sense of treating men as things and not as persons, that people will either learn that they can do without it, or that when a few destroy it with 'creative violence', showing that its apparent vast strength is, in fact, but a brittle rigidity, there will be found no need to replace it: spontaneous co-operation will follow. Anarchism would seem a minor and discredited theory of the future, but for its sudden reinvention by 'revolutionary socialists' among students all over the world in the late 1960s. It is not an especially plausible prophecy, but it does furnish, in however deranged a form, a good testimony to individual human freedom and a bad report on what our contemporary society can do by way of fulfilling, in a just and stable manner, the perennial problem of government: the reconciliation of order with freedom.[68]

*   *   *

Put in this way, it is always inherently unlikely that humanity will settle for any one solution. But we do not need to lose respect and tolerance for any plausible solutions simply because we happen to praise one more than another. It is still likely that the future will be better than the past for most of humanity, but unlikely that fundamentally new forms of government will arise. It is unlikely that there will be a world government, but equally unlikely, looking especially at Africa, Western Europe, Eastern Europe, South America, the Middle East and South-East Asia, that such a multitude of small states will continue all claiming to be sovereign. Between the one and the other there are a large number of possible relationships of mutual dependence and co-operation, as well as of particular forms of partial independence, few of which have yet emerged clearly, but many of which soon will.

PART TWO

A Model of the Elementary Types of Government

---

14. THE PROBLEM

So far I have offered a highly simplified but reasonably comprehensive historical sketch. Other categories could be used, and many sub-divisions. The categories I have used are fairly ordinary terms such as historians cannot avoid using, however much they stress the uniqueness of events. But they are based on usage, not on any theories of what constitute the significant relations in government. Perhaps implicit in this, however, is something more systematic and more clearly based on true theory.

Ever so many schemes of classification of 'types of government' exist, and much slightly more tendentious talk and writing about 'typologies' and 'political systems'. The framing and criticism of such schemes has become almost an established branch of the academic study of politics, and everyone can supply to taste their own footnotes full of examples of such work, both empirical (that is typologies purporting to be theories or generalisations) and analytical (that is, true by definition or internal coherence, usually called 'model building'), and – perhaps more often than either alone – philosophically bewildering mixtures of the two. Are there any grounds on which we can rationally prefer one scheme to another? Are there, to think of common faults, empirical schemes which are not so concrete that they lose all generality (i.e. that there are a thousand and one types of government), not yet so general that they are only models of some reformed or deformed world (i.e. 'ideal types') but not of the actual?

What, after all, are we classifying for anyway? It is necessary to ask this if one is to find some middle path of mutual comprehension between being too systematic and not systematic enough (between, speaking broadly, both the Marxist and the American behavioural schools, on the one hand, and the British and the modern German empirical schools on the other).

There are some radical nominalists who would think that every system of government is *sui generis* – and they are right, of course, in respect of certain questions. We are unlikely to glean many answers from comparisons or generalisations to questions about the fall of Walpole, the rise of the Pelhams, the formation of Aberdeen's last ministry or the resignation of Macmillan. But other sorts of questions (say about the growth of party bureaucracy or of central planning) can hardly be answered without generalisation or comparison. The distinction is not a logical one, or one between 'persons', 'events' or 'social forces' (all different ways of looking at the same things), but simply one between degrees of importance or triviality. And here we can do nothing but recognise that while 'importance' and 'triviality' may be definable in terms of influence on events, they are also – thank God – completely subjective according to what scholars, inventors, scientists, statesmen and lovers (or in other words, anyone) happen to be interested in. I may simply happen to be interested in 'War Games' or the Common Seal of Canada for their own sakes – unlikely but possible.

All I think we can and should take for granted is that classifications which deserve to be commonly used must answer important questions. 'Importance' is then some guarantee of some degree of generality. For otherwise it might sensibly be said – as so many textbooks appear to exhibit – that we simply classify for convenience. The number of instances of unique governments (the extreme nominalist position) are so many that we have to adopt some, or any, more or less arbitrary (and let us not pretend that they are anything but arbitrary, etc.) scheme of classification. Again, this view is not to be dismissed out of hand. It is at least wise to treat classifications as extremely tentative, even if not as purely arbitrary. Yet this view has one great disadvantage. I think in each case it could be shown, a wearisome if pointed exercise, not to be true. For every different classification answers, consciously or unconsciously, implicitly or explicitly, different questions about different aspects of society. People classify for a purpose, and these purposes have to be ascertained. Some of these purposes are highly moralistic. For instance, most people, if the problem arises at all, operate with 'good' and 'bad', or with 'free government' and (a great variety of abusive words) 'the rest'. And, of course, such classifications have their uses. Other classifications strive to be ethically neutral, so that, for instance, whether countries have constitutions or not becomes significant – and an endless source of reverberating quibbles about what 'constitution' means. Many classifications, probably most, are inspired by some political doctrine attempting to blend the *is* and the *ought* (one cannot conceive of a political doctrine which did not offer grounds as to why what is held to be desirable was not also possible). For instance, to give only broad examples, the liberal tends to classify states by their type of electoral and representative institutions (by which there are then some naughty governments which are scarcely states at all); the conservative by the character of the ruling elite, and the socialist by the degree of working-class control of the economy (and if the criteria do not appear to fit, then so much the worse for these states – morally – or else they are deemed to be, a much better bet, unstable – empirically).

So my first simple-minded point is that we are very unlikely to find any interesting or important classifications which do not contain both some moralistic element (i.e. one would like these distinctions to hold) *and* some empirical elements (i.e. that these distinctions have held). Every different classification answers, consciously or not, different questions about differing aspects of politics. There are institutional classifications, there are classifications by systems of authority and legitimacy; there are modern attempts to correlate either, or both, to types of social structure; and there are economic and even allegedly psychological classifications. Usually some kind of neo-Cartesian separation between 'ideas' and 'institutions' is assumed, and the bridges between them are then called 'processes' – and to some the world is nothing but 'process': there is neither fire nor pot, but only boiling; and there are no points of departure or final resting places, but only travelling (though they then have to identify many sorts of process all with strange patent names). And all of these new inventions stay together if put together, but there seem no compelling reasons why we should ever adopt one rather than another.

Every classification, then, serves some purpose, though usually very limited purposes either connected with some moral doctrine or with those aspects of society which any particular scholar happens to find interesting.

I take the simple view that it is most helpful to use traditional words which embrace the largest numbers of different questions – questions perhaps initially of intellectual convenience only, but which must finally be shown to be of political importance. To ask questions is to assume that answers can be given in terms of theories – that is explanations based upon generalisations; but note that the theories are never wholly distinct from doctrines – that is what ought to be and could be the case. Those who hold, for instance, that the most important question is to ask what kind of political elite or ruling class a society has, must also believe that to study that elite is to explain the main factors in the rise and fall of societies; and they will almost always, not surprisingly, hold strong opinions, explicitly or implicitly, about the desirability or not of elites in general.

15. QUESTIONS, ANSWERS AND THEORIES

So I set out initially just to identify the range of questions which have traditionally been asked about forms of government in political literature. 'Questions', but, of course, each of these following questions can, if thought to be the only significant question (as each of them has by some writers who have in fact done reasonably useful work), be treated as *the unique answer*. It should be obvious that there are no such single answers, even though people have believed that there are. But it is not so obvious, as I think I can show, that the questions deemed to be significant each yield a different answer in relation to possible or actual situations, and that all these answers fall into three broad clusters which are readily named. If the relationships between them do not necessarily constitute a 'system', yet they are, apparently, systematic.

Eleven subjects for questions appear to dominate both the traditional and the modern literature of politics. I do not claim that they are all either logically or pragmatically distinct, a different reading would define them differently and produce a different number. But I do claim that such a list as this is reasonably precise and exhaustive, and the answers to further significant questions would be unlikely to involve the discovery or definition of new types of government.

Questions have been asked which have assumed the dominant importance of each of these categories: (i) the role of the inhabitants;[69] (ii) the official doctrine;[70] (iii) the typical social structure;[71] (iv) the character and composition of the elite group;[72] (v) the typical institution of government;[73] (vi) the type of economy;[74] (vii) rights of property;[75] (viii) the prevalent attitudes to law;[76] (ix) attitudes to knowledge;[77] (x) attitudes to the diffusion of information;[78] and (xi) attitudes to politics (or 'opposition', 'contestation' or 'public and legitimate conflict') itself.[79]

What I want to suggest is that while the role and interaction of these categories of question and answer will vary uniquely for any particular society or system of government, they are still all present in any known or seriously attempted form of government; and that these forms of governments are basically, if reduced to their elements without contingent embellishments, three. I would name the three simply: autocratic, republican and totalitarian government, and offer these – as it were – premature definitions.

'Autocratic' I take as either the government of an autocrat ('tyrant', 'despot', 'chieftain', 'king' or 'emperor' all being associated words of local and varying shades of meaning) or of an autocracy ('aristocracy', 'oligarchy', 'theocracy', 'bureaucracy', 'military caste', etc.). There is, at this level of generality, no significant difference of behaviour between regimes ruled by a few or by one. The oldest authorities agreed on this. Aristotle's 'Monarchy' is really an empty class, or a theoretical speculation – though admittedly one more real to the Greeks than to us: *if* there was a perfect man then he should be made king, for a perfect man was clearly a god. (His distinction only helps us, even in modern times, to understand why some great autocrats have acted as if they were literally superhuman.) Machiavelli's dramatised 'Prince' turns out in the *Discourses*, more soberly and yet even more powerfully, to be princely power (or absolute power), a function of government which republicans can even (or especially *should*) embrace who have not lost their *virtú* (political guts). And Hobbes also makes quite clear that the power of Leviathan can be found in one or in many. *Autocracy*, to anticipate from what follows, *is then the form of government which attempts to solve the basic problem of the adjustment of order to diversity by the authoritative enforcement of one of the diverse interests (whether seen as material or moral – almost always, in fact, both) as an officially sponsored and static ideology.*

'Republican' (or following Aristotle strictly, 'political governments' or 'polities', that is those who accept and even honour

70

politics rather than trying either to suppress it, or to surpass it) is a far more comprehensive and accurate term than 'democratic'. There were republics long before the majority of inhabitants became enfranchised, and if 'democracy' is taken to mean something like government by the consent of the majority, then this is true for *any* modern state: the Soviets and the Chinese, unlike ancient and even early-modern (i.e. pre-industrial) autocrats, are as desperately dependent on the consent of the majority as are the Americans or the Swiss. That this consent may be due to force, chicane or lack of genuine choice is another matter (only confusing if one sees a necessary, rather than a desirable, but far from inevitable, connection between democracy and freedom). The point is that all industrial or industrialising regimes must (because of their dependence on the skilled factory worker) be democratic in a sense that autocracies facing vast peasantries had no need. And if the Americans, to speak broadly, have debased the word 'democracy' into almost total uselessness as a scientific term, the French tradition of 'republic', to speak with equal pedantry, has made us forget the Roman, the British Whig and the Dutch traditions in which 'republican virtues' and 'republican institutions' certainly did not imply 'no king', still less a dead one. So *Republican government,* to anticipate from what follows, *is then the attempt to solve the basic problem of the adjustment to diversity by conciliating differing interests by letting them share in the government or in the competitive choosing of the government.*

'Totalitarian' may appear to beg many questions, and is a term, for different reasons, almost impossible to use in some company, but if it is taken as a category of aspiration, not of performance, then I think events in this century have shown its persistent plausibility. Thus it rests on a different basis as a classifying term than 'autocracy' and 'republican', both of which, no one could deny, describe many actual present and past situations. But even if, which I accept, indeed claim (*pace* some passages in Hannah Arendt and most in Carl Friedrick), no modern government has actually been able to exercise total power, yet it is necessary to recognise that the idea has arisen, that many conditions of the modern world make it plausible, that it has been tried and could well be tried again. If actual societies show no pattern of total government power, great events

71

have occurred which can only be explained as consequences of the attempt to control totally or to keep alive such a hope. It is a peculiarity of the modern world (stemming from a belief in inevitable progress) that a category of aspiration, not subject to immediate empirical validation, becomes relevent as a classification. That some prophecies can now seek to be self-validating is now predictable enough. Arendt, Friedrich and others have argued the unique primacy of ideology in 'totalitarian states', which is true, but it does not make these states in fact total in their control of their inhabitants. Perhaps what should really emerge is a formulation even more abstract than 'ideology', but psychologically even more compelling : the uniqueness to the modern world of 'consciousness', as Marx and Hegel argued, that ideas and circumstances are both uniquely related to each other, are knowable and thus manipulable. Consciousness, breaking from habit and tradition, alone constitutes both the necessary condition of morality and the possibility of controlled social change (or predictable progress towards a definite and final social goal) – itself a distinctively modern concept. To come down to earth, were autocrats conscious of governing autocratically? I very much doubt, except in pejorative moral senses. Did they see themselves as deliberately operating a specific system, or merely as simply governing? But the Nazis, the Soviets and the new Chinese have all, in very different ways, been stridently explicit about *trying* (whereas the Italians and the Spanish merely pretended) to do something new and comprehensive. ('Politics' itself they denounced as selfish, as something not of or in the general interest; or they have defined it, correctly, as being concerned with partial interests and relative truths and not with 'the truth' and the total management of society and a general or mass welfare). To those who see the whole concept of totalitarianism (rather than its abuse) as simply a product of 'the cold war', I would say that we all should, indeed, have been railing against the impossibility of totalitarianism more than its iniquity; but that it is after all what has happened in Russia and Germany (and may be happening in China), precisely the attempt to do the impossible which has killed men in millions where the autocrats killed in their tens of thousands. So *Totalitarian government*, to anticipate from what follows, *is the attempt to solve the basic problem of the adjust-*

72

ment of order to diversity by creating a completely new society such that conflict would no longer arise: it attempts to do this by means of guidance and enforcement of a revolutionary ideology which claims to be scientific, thus comprehensive and necessary, both for knowledge and allegiance.

I suggest that these definitions are premature in the sense that their validity depends not on their familiarity and customary usage, but that empirically each of them yields a different answer to the dominant questions set out above. Am I finding the categories to fit the concepts, or vice versa? What I think I have done is to ask the above questions of all types of government of which I have ever read, then to find that the answers fall into three clusters consistent with the above *a priori* (as set down above) or traditional (with the exception of 'totalitarian') concepts.

16. THE THREE PATTERNS

So, very *briefly* and *schematically*, let me try to show the apparent pattern or clustering of particular answers to general questions (otherwise it is 800 pages, if it proves, after criticism, worth trying to show the sources and authorities – which would be all very traditional and conventional – for this rather obvious classification).

(i) *The Role of the Inhabitants*

AUTOCRATIC: *passive obedience and social deference* ('suffer the powers that be' and 'the rich man in his castle, the poor man at his gate . . .'); but then general mobilisation is impossible.

REPUBLICAN: *voluntary and individual participation* ('republican virtues' and 'active citizenship' are required, but hence a man is free to act as a citizen or not; so a discriminatory or a partial kind of loyalty: only in time of war can the state mobilise all its inhabitants, and in other times any individual can, but some must, move backwards and forwards between private and public life).

TOTALITARIAN: *mass participation and compulsory explicit enthusiasm* (passive obedience is rejected as inadequate or suspect: 'Who are those who are not the friends of the people but that they are enemies of the people?'). Precisely because 'the system' is a system, all must move as one.

(ii) *The Official Doctrine*

AUTOCRATIC: allegiance is *a religious duty and government is part of divine order* (when the basis of political legitimacy is

74

made transcendental and beyond question : Gibbon's sneer, 'the usefulness of christianity to civil polity', deserves to be generalised. And if this sounds like a piece of Enlightenment or Victorian rationalism, it is : I think they were right on this point – though the converse does not necessarily hold, that religion is dependent on autocracy. Now the only possible proof of this generalisation, like all the generalisations I am recounting, is not any listing of authorities however vast, *but whether it is possible to think of an actual contrary instance.* Nonetheless only open disbelief is punished (inner reservations to the doctrine are tolerated if they remain private).

REPUBLICAN : allegiance is demanded and given *on utilitarian and secular grounds* (when practical benefits in the here-and-now must be demonstrated : if authority is not precisely a contract, yet a contractual language of 'rights and duties' is spoken). Nonetheless, occasional conformity (though often trivial) is demanded to each particular formulation of the doctrine.

TOTALITARIAN : allegiance is *ideological* (when it is supposed to be all-embracing, exclusive and predetermined for necessary purposes, since all thought is a *product* of circumstances – whether material or racial – so that only when all social contradictions are completely removed, the task of the revolution, is a single truth possible). Inner reservations must be exposed and punished just as surely as open dissent.

(iii) *Typical Social Structure*

AUTOCRATIC : *a highly stratified caste or class structure* usually involving some slavery or serfdom.

REPUBLICAN : a large *middle-class or bourgeoisie* (on this all authorities, despite difficulties of definition, are agreed, from Aristotle, Machiavelli, Montesquieu, Harrington and Marx to modern political sociologists like Kornhauser or Lipset). But note that 'middle', in modern conditions, need not imply that other classes exist : the classless society, when it comes, will be bourgeois in its structure and values – not proletarian. 'Proletarian' is a category of oppression, not of dominance : the 'dictatorship of the proletariat' inevitably becomes that of, at the best, a 'new class'.

75

TOTALITARIAN: *egalitarian* in aspiration, possibly the halfway fraud of 'national equality' (but in fact a social-structure mainly determined by political function).

(iv) *Elite Group*

AUTOCRATIC: *self-perpetuating and exclusive* (almost always fortified by myths, biological or religious, of descent from gods or great men). Relatively small in numbers.

REPUBLICAN: *a stable political class enjoying social prestige*, but not exclusively, and readily penetrable by candidates from political and educational institutions designed to encourage mobility (then always the political and especially the democratic argument turns around, 'how much mobility?' – but always some). Relatively large in numbers.

TOTALITARIAN: in theory *a meritocracy based on perfect social mobility* ('to each according to his needs, from each according to his abilities'). In practice a relatively small and self-perpetuating 'inner party' with a relatively large 'outer party'.

(v) *Typical Institution of Government*

AUTOCRATIC: *the Court or the Palace* (a visible, physically locatable, militarily defendable awe-inspiring but *isolated* and private society within a society: the place where an inner aristocracy resides permanently, or where all the aristocracy has to reside occasionally. There may be rival courts in some types of autocracy, particularly the feudal, but it is always regarded as unnatural and temporary. 'Come ye not to Court? To whose Court, to the King's Court or to Hampton Court?').

REPUBLICAN: *a Parliament, Assembly, or Congress* (sometimes by which, but more often through which, the country can only be governed). They are usually built in centres of population.

TOTALITARIANISM: the *single party* (who function as both the elite group and the ideologists who can foretell the future development of the ideology through changing circumstances. Note that a single party with a genuine ideology is a quite different institution from any single party, even the overwhelmingly dominant one, in states with public contestation be-

76

tween parties – which is the usual, but not the invariable, pattern of republics). Surviving autocracies all claim to have parties, but this is very rarely true : African political parties, for instance, have often turned out to be personal followings, which could not outlive their leader, with – the vital point – no powers of self-perpetuation such as totalitarian parties enjoy.

(vi) *The Economy*

AUTOCRATIC : *agrarian* (and if a relatively large country, almost invariably either following a theory of 'autarky' or involved in constant political and military attempts to dominate markets and sources of supplies). Certainly *pre-industrial* : industrialism tends either to lead into one of the other categories, or results in chronic instability for autocracies.

REPUBLICAN : originally a *market or capitalist economy, finally a 'mixed economy'* (that is self-consciously mixed, as a matter of public policy; fully and rationally planned economies do not exist, the aspiration towards them only arose from the experience of the First World War – even to Marx production was either a product of class interest or else, after the great qualitative changes, would be spontaneous; but to put an economy on a war-time footing of total planning usually demands war, whether internal or external).

TOTALITARIAN : *the war-economy* or planned and *rapid* industrialisation (the rejection of 'mere' economic criteria).

(vii) *Theories of Property*

AUTOCRATIC : the visible mark of *status*, hence land (with the personal subservience it implies from tenants or serfs), treasure and arms are all god-given to the rulers, and it is for no man to question their incidence. But it is recognised that every inhabitant must have a minimum of the stable food grown from land : famine must be avoided prudentially by rulers, and anyway is a sign of divine collective punishment.

REPUBLICAN : the visible mark of *worthiness* – originally moral and economic endeavour are not clearly distinguished. God distributes the prizes but does not weight the runners. Even in

77

secular forms, however, a man must justify his attainment of property by merit and his retention of it by use (cf. John Locke's mixing property with labour and using it to the common good – at least not using it against the common good). Forms of property become ever more mobile and individual: from land to houses and workshops, then to joint-stock shares, then to educationally acquired skills. The social problem of property moves from ownership to control.

TOTALITARIAN: no *personal property* – in theory – except the minimum of furniture, apparel and cleaning materials; personal property is the mark of class differention. But in fact a series of properties in rights and privileges, by virtue of party or bureaucratic function, for special services; but not assignable, they terminate with the job (whereas in Republics the view grows, or lingers from previous types of property, that if an educationally acquired skill cannot be used, the person should be compensated as of right). Control of property is made difficult by myths of popular or universal ownership of everything.

(viii) *Attitude to Law*

AUTOCRATIC: *customary and god-given*: the law *is* the state, both indistinguishable and both (officially) unchangeable. (Autocracies, history was invented to tell us, are founded by gods, demi-gods or supermen who *give* the thus sacred laws. More mundanely, the actual law that is applied to individuals will be a product of their status, and the lower their status, the more arbitrary it will be in application, timing and outcome).

REPUBLICAN: both *custom and statute* (parliaments as makers of *new* laws, but greatly limited by custom and convention, particularly in *how* they make law. So both 'the good old laws' and 'the will of the state'. Law between individuals is largely a matter of contract and its application is regular or general, but invariably slow even if reasonably predictable). A balance is struck between tradition and the deliberate creation of new economic and social relationships.

TOTALITARIAN: *laws of history* (to be interpreted by party ideologists, who themselves have varying degrees of conviction, but all believe that some parts of the ideology constitute necessary

78

laws of social development). Actual law is interpreted by its intention, not by what it says; to be 'law abiding' is not enough, is even seen as deceitful – a man must live up to the spirit of the laws. And the law is arbitrary and swift in application, but regular and general in outcome if applied.

(ix) *Attitudes to Knowledge*

AUTOCRATIC : all knowledge is seen as one and as part of the hidden *'mystery of power'* or inexplicable *'reason of state'* (to be accepted on authority, if questioned at all then only among – and often for the entertainment of – the ruling elite, so within the palace walls); hence *censorship* as a general (but negative) institution (if there are universities or learned academies, they are part of the court circle). Knowledge is power and is to be guarded jealously.

REPUBLICAN : *knowledge is fragmented*, most moral truths become seen as relative (and distinguished from scientific truths), and all moral truths become open to some form of *public questioning*; further, there is official patronage of independent or semi-independent institutions of learning (there will be censorship, but of a residual, limited and negative kind). Knowledge has to be spread for this kind of society to work effectively. In other words, it is no longer believed that knowledge constitutes a unity, moral truths are distinguished from scientific truths and the 'ought' from the 'is' ('two things never cease to move me with wonder, the starry heavens above and the moral law within', said Emmanuel Kant); and it is recognised that most moral truths are in their particular forms relative to circumstances, and that everything can be publicly and critically discussed.

TOTALITARIAN : all knowledge is seen as one and is *ideological* : the censorship is general (as in autocracy), but it is also positive : *propaganda becomes a state institution*. (Universities and academies are under complete party control, and science is seen only as technology.) Knowledge is graded according to recognised degrees of ideological awareness, and at the appropriate level its acquisition is compulsory.

(x) *Attitudes to the Diffusion of Information*

AUTOCRATIC : Proclamations, but no regular news, hence *rumour*

79

and gossip as institutions (used and exploited by both rulers and ruled), hence both the spy as eavesdropper, who reports what people say, and the satirist or wise-buffoon also become institutionalised. (So mainly oral communication, but some private circulation of manuscripts about how things happen, or should happen. If these 'Books of Power' come to be printed, or otherwise made readily available, it is a sign that republican conditions are beginning to arise : the prince himself is needing to know more accurately how people and forces beyond his immediate control will react, and authors think that there are useful allies outside the Palace.) The truth cannot be told about how the regime works (hence only a covert or allegorical study of politics).

REPUBLICAN : *newspapers* and a growingly popular market for them, some at least not under the control of the state. (Printed materials outpace oral communication, whether rumours or speeches, both in quantity and accuracy as sources of political information and speculation.) The effective working of these regimes comes to depend on more and more people having access to accurate information about how the state is run and on the state being able to measure public opinion reasonably accurately; hence considerable neutrality and objectivity in official publications, polls and surveys in democratic republics and a thriving literature of politics – both in treatises and novels.

TOTALITARIAN : *mass-communications* controlled completely by the party and a compulsory market for them. (The encyclopaedia and the newspaper preferred to the book, and novels specifically, but all other art forms generally, are required to be propaganda. No objective studies of politics, and hence extreme unreliability of all kinds of official statistics – even for the party's own use – and no reliable knowledge of public opinion.)

(xi) *Attitudes to Politics*

AUTOCRATIC : either *above politics*, or politics is *limited* to the secrecy of the Palace or the Court (conflict and opposition are always expected, and sometimes tolerated, so long as they do not become public or appeal to a public outside the ruling class). Politics is conspiracy.

REPUBLICAN : *politics is always tolerated*, sometimes encouraged, and opposition can be made public and is sometimes institutionalised. Politics is conciliation.

TOTALITARIAN : *politics and opposition are seen as subversive*, and not just personal intrigue or conspiracy, but a symptom of social contradictions yet to be eradicated. Politics is a bourgeois sham.

* * *

Perhaps it is needless to say that I cannot give to purely economic theories (whether of the Marxist or the liberal kind) that overriding importance which many attach to them. To ask what kind of theories have been seriously advanced, and look at least plausible, is to see at once that many general factors enter into any sensible explanation of the rise and fall of political and social systems. Marxism is a highly relevant theory of industrial societies, but Marx's writings were extremely thin and *a priori* about pre-industrial forms; and it is over-ingenious and purely pietistic labour to try to show what he might have said about things he never really considered. Before the industrial revolution, economic motivation was simply less important and economies were inherently less systematic and less subject to effective controls. If I seem to adopt a comprehensive 'political interpretation', it is only because political and moral factors obviously enter into any assessment of the relative importance of different theories, although the existence of the theories themselves is objective enough. Politics accepts relative truths : ideological explanations all hope for a truth of truths.

17. CONCLUSIONS AND DIFFICULTIES

My contention is that this scheme is not just analytically simple, but is empirically true: that these types of government, studied historically (including contemporary history), reveal these broad characteristics; and also that these characteristics, if the questions they answer separately are put together, are in some way systematically related – as best expressed by the three main concepts. One should reach the same results whichever way one works. This is, of course, too neat by far. The characteristics are themselves generalisations of a considerable degree of abstraction, like any generalisations, so liable to particular exceptions and peculiar and famous hybrids at any given time and place. But the argument comes down to this (if advanced in full): to convince the historian that generalisation is sensible and that any generalisation involves simplification or abstraction; and to convince the political scientist that these apparent systematic relationships can be expressed thus simply – without any more elaborate conceptual framework or any special vocabulary of induced (i.e. quite unknown to the actors in political events) processes.

What I have not done, of course, is to *explain* these relationships – which is a huge and perhaps impossible task. What is the precise relationship, for instance between the questions of the role of the inhabitant and of the elite groups (see (i) and (iv) above) or of the typical social structure and of attitudes to politics (see (iii) *and* (xi) *above*). I would simply assume that there is *some* systematic relationship: to treat them all as independent variables would seem mildly crazy; but so would it be to claim that they are all necessarily dependent on each other (still more that one could ever express these relationships quantitatively although one doubtless could symbolically).

Perhaps what is most worrying is what one may mean by

'systematic' and still more by 'system'. But if my attempt to summarise traditional knowledge is acceptable, if the generalisations appear to be broadly true, perhaps we need not worry too much about this. If we say that there is a political system or a social system, we are saying that every factor in it interacts with, conditions and is conditioned by everything else. (Hence to say either 'political' or 'social' will not matter very much *if* there is such a system : we are only singling out, rather improperly and tendentiously, what we think to be a particularly important factor, but not one in any sense autonomous.) Now I think this to be true of anything one can sensibly call a society. It sounds silly even to bother to say this, because it is really a truism. In societies everything does interact (albeit for many things quite trivially). But it is worth saying because often the concept of 'system' is a tautology : simply what we mean by society, or by societies as they appear when we study them. Economic theory, for instance, assumes that there is an economic system : but then some economists are for ever complaining that political factors spoil the rationality of the assumed economic system (and this can be said by both liberals and Marxists, though by no one else). I think we can properly be more empirical than economists, even at the price of being less systematic. But this does not mean that we need be unsystematic.

If, then, 'system' is a truism or a tautology, no inferences can be drawn from any particular formulation. We must draw concepts of 'system' from what we observe, not vice versa. Suppose we ask, is it true in fact that everything important interacts, conditions or is conditioned by everything else in the political or social system? The answer is obviously not. 'Importance' makes the difference. To vary factor 'X' within a social system may have effects on all the other factors, but many of them are almost certain to be trivial. And I do not see how much further one can go than this : some criteria of importance must be introduced into any systematic analysis of politics. Usually these criteria are themselves political. I do not see how this can be avoided, nor really why it should be. I have tried to show elsewhere the close and inevitable connection between political theories and political doctrines. What is important for science is not that the motive is pure, but that the particular generalisation is of such a kind that it can be confirmed or refuted.

If my generalisations are mainly true, some important systematic relationships appear – as I will soon briefly show. But a final double objection against wishing for too high a degree of abstraction, however internally consistent the theory then appears – the neo-Parsonian 'systems analysis' approach. Firstly, it is unnecessary, seeing how much one can draw together with simpler, traditional methods; and secondly, strictly speaking if there were a fully interdependent social system, there would be no politics. This was, indeed, famously the view of Marx, and on a methodological level, is that of Parsons too. Is politics just a derivative of all other social relations, as some sociologists argue, or is it that which alone holds, by will and reason, any society together – as Hobbes argued?

Such extreme views are probably not very helpful. Government arises because there is no spontaneously operating relationship between social groups such as to ensure their continuity and survival without political skill or invention. Social structure is never completely systematic (except in misleading models of society): it is government that, at the very least, picks up the loose ends, improvises connections for those that have broken, and hammers or oils others into easier motion. No amount of political skill can transform some situations, but none uniquely *determine* any form of government. All one could say is that the difficulties get progressively greater, practically overwhelming, if the prince or autocrat, fortunate in war, wishes to govern a state whose, say, (i), (iii), (vi) and (ix) are all more usually associated with, broadly speaking, republican government.

If political sociology were simply a reduction of politics to sociology it would be either (as it sometimes is) an unhelpful abstract and overly systematic way of looking at things, or else empirically false. The real question, at this level of abstraction, is always a double one: 'How far are types of government determined by social structure?'; *and* 'How far is social structure determined by government?'

All this as postscript or interjection because I am so conscious of fighting on a double-front: against those who see no use in any such systematic analysis as I have sketched out above, and against those who might say either that it is not systematic enough (that is not quantifiable), or (the objection that worries me more) too specific and concrete.

What, of importance, follows from such an analysis? If the eleven different clusterings within three types are even broadly correct empirically, it argues considerable stability for any regime when they coincide. I did not set out to set down the conditions of political stability: this may be the master question, but then there are obviously many conditions common to any possible forms of government. (Hence the longer list of conditions for the stability of 'political regimes' or republics in the Appendix to the Pelican edition of my *In Defence of Politics*.) But it would seem that subsuming all other classifications which answer different questions, such as 'empire' (the rule of one culture over another which can occur in all three forms), or sub-categories of any one form, like oriental despotism and feudal government as distinct types of autocratic rule, the tendency is for states to be somewhere firmly within these three clusterings, or else to be unstable.

This is why all the attempts to define what is so obvious a question in the modern world prove futile – the distinct form of government of the New Nations, the Emergent Territories, the Third World and other names. They have no distinct form. It is either romantic of us or ultra-sociological to think, as so many think, that they necessarily must. Simply take governments in former British, Belgian and French Africa – their most common characteristic is chronic instability. The social systems seem largely independent of the political. The governments would like to transform society, sometimes even they have a totalitarian impulse, but they have no possibility of succeeding in that way. They are mainly autocracies, but rendered unstable by aroused economic expectations both in their elites and in their general populations – expectations arising from completely external factors and which cannot possibly be met internally. This does argue, it is hard to avoid the conclusion, that the long-term effects of the industrial and the French revolutions have been (as our liberal ancestors said) to render autocratic government less and less viable, though to make totalitarian government a tempting aspiration, and in some circumstances almost as plausible as republican government would be.

There is some case for calling all these many different types of government 'transitional government' or some such equivocal term; but this is only to lump together as a classification what is, in fact, a problem or a dilemma. It is indeed very hard to show what systematic relationships these new governments all have in common, especially when their problems mainly arise, taken one by one, from their lack as yet (or else utter collapse, which in some cases is possible) of sufficient coherence between political and social structure. Even David Apter's concept of 'modernising autocracies' confuses, I think, a problem, a dilemma, an aspiration with genuinely systematic political relationships. The above analysis would suggest that a 'modernising autocracy' is a contradiction in terms, or something which must overcome (and then probably in the one direction or the other), if it is to have any hopes of permanence, substantial 'internal contradictions'.

This is why 'democracy' is unhelpful as a classification of systems of government. It is a common condition of all industrial or industrialising governments (and has nothing necessarily to do with personal freedom). Modern republican government (that is post-industrial revolution) and totalitarian government both depend upon and need to mobilise the energies of the mass of their population in a way that autocracies cannot. And 'nationalism' as a doctrine has no more proved a sufficient condition for stability in new states than it has proved a necessary condition for stability in all old states. (To avoid misunderstanding let me underline one point: it seemed to me historically wrong to make a competitive party system a necessary condition for republican government; and it is also wrong in the modern world: Tanzania, for instance, must fall squarely under my republican criteria, so must Yugoslavia and several of the Peoples' Republics in Eastern Europe would seem to be moving that way were it not for Soviet military power.) So my analysis makes me both pessimistic and optimistic. That some regimes which are at present autocratic systems will have to become more and more republican in form in order to industrialise or to apply industrial methods to agriculture; but also that others may try, with outside help, the path of total transformation. A rather obvious prophecy emerges: an increased polarisation between 'republican' and 'totalitarian' systems of government, so long as one grants that persistent instability will be the lot, for many many years, of many governments in new nations.

The actual advantages of republics in survival and the tempting prospects of totalitarianism in permanence are plainly bound up with their superior capacity, compared to autocracies,

86

to institutionalise change – whether by self-generating processes, by state planning or the far more ordinary mixtures of both. Stability, in other words, is not a static category. Renewal and adjustment to changing circumstances is the test of stable government, not simply longevity : consider, for example, the incredibly tenuous, but seventy-year life-span, of the French Third Republic – simply, as the late Professor Alfred Cobban put it, 'its failure to collapse'. And I think I am plagiarising from an American student's seminar paper when I say that 'political stability is a process of organising change so as to ensure future self-sustaining change without serious institutional rupture'. Yes.

One last objection to my proposed classification, an historical thesis to my mind more telling than Third World objections : Wittfogel's magisterial correction of, or polemic against, Marx, that there was, in 'oriental despotism', a pre-industrial form of total power. If so, this would completely shatter the sharp distinction drawn between old autocracy and aspirant totalitarianism; and any systematic relationships between the eleven categories would be in doubt. They would be in doubt if all that followed for government and society from the need for vast schemes of hydraulic engineering for irrigation was as Wittfogel asserts.

Certainly this kind of despotism or autocratic rule could be more arbitrary, and thus powerful and unpredictable, than modern totalitarianism. But misuse of individuals is not the sole test of totalitarianism : one can readily concede that cruelties in these ancient regimes are more horrible, because seemingly more pointless and arbitrary and done with less sublime excuse. Yet one must add that such arbitrary cruelties and enforced labour were probably even less efficient than in Hitler's Germany or Stalin's Russia where the enthusiasm of large parties was evident and effective.

Certainly the scale of public works and the organisation of it by the state surpasses, in Wittfogel's regimes, anything else in the annals of autocracy. They are a very special sub-category. But a sub-category nonetheless, for Wittfogel is surely wrong in his key assertion. Total power is only a very relative thing if it does not involve, as it has even in republics under conditions of modern war, total mobilisation of manpower. Hydraulic planning was vast and great planning, involving the conscription and forced labour of tens and even hundreds of thousand of peasants.

87

But the key institution was what he himself calls, by analogy, the *corvée*. It was a conscription of individuals or a mobilisation of society only for certain seasons of the year for the essential public works of irrigation. Actual production of food remained, if not private, at least communal at a village level. Hence a segmented society. Production was not controlled by the state as in modern regimes. If the armies of canal diggers and ditchers were kept from the villages for even one whole year, famine for the entire society would have followed. Only in industrial society, only through the factory and through specialisation, can workers be conscripted in such a way that the actual exercise of total power does not result in total disruption and general starvation. But even so, it is necessary to remind ourselves that the third category is a category of aspiration: it has yet to be proved, in Russia or China, that agriculture can be fully industrialised or communised and the peasantry transformed or got rid of utterly.

Lastly, I stress 'elementary': many sub-categories are possible, and many questions are important that cut across these three categories completely. But if 'elementary', elementary in the sense of basic, not of simple: of *grundlagen,* not of abstract models – even 'elemental', for it seems plain that there are strong causal connections between many of these categories, so that the three types of government constitute 'fields of force' which tend to exclude other alternatives and, in the long run, draw marginal cases one way or another towards the centre of one of the three constellations. This does have obvious implications for political practice – as Machiavelli long ago saw: if one is concerned with survival, then it is clearly one thing or another: intermediate positions prove fatal. Personally I doubt if one can go much further than this, for instance to say which of the eleven categories are the more open to deliberate control. This will probably vary greatly, as will their mutual importance, according to different circumstances and culture-patterns. At this point answers become very specific. But it is something to have tried to go so far as I have tried to go in summarising a conventional wisdom which is far more systematic than is now generally believed, for: 'Though nothing can be immortal, which mortals make, yet if man had the use of reason they pretend to, their Commonwealths might be secured at least from perishing by internal diseases.' (Thomas Hobbes.)

88

REFERENCES

1. A. R. Radcliffe-Brown, *African Political Systems*, ed. Fortes, Meyer and Evans-Pritchard (Oxford University Press, 1961).
2. B. Malinowski, *Scientific Theory of Culture* (Allen & Unwin, 1947).
3. Lucy Mair, *Primitive Government* (Penguin Books, 1962).
4. R. H. Lowie, *The Origin of the State* (New York : Harcourt Brace, 1927).
5. L. Krader, *The Formation of the State* (Englewood Cliffs, N.J. : Prentice-Hall, 1968). But in contrast consider the more complex societies described in Jack Goody (ed.), *Succession to High Office*, Cambridge Papers in Social Anthropology (Cambridge University Press, 1966; Englewood Cliffs, N.J. : Prentice-Hall, 1969).
6. Max Gluckman, *Politics, Law and Ritual in Tribal Society* (Oxford : Blackwell, 1965).
7. Robert G. Wesson, *The Imperial Order* (Berkeley and Los Angeles : University of California Press, 1967) is an essential but under-used book on which I have leant heavily.
8. Max Weber, *The Religion of China* (Glencoe Ill. : Free Press, 1951).
9. S. M. Eisenstadt, *The Political System of Empires* (Glencoe, Ill. : Free Press, 1963).
10. Sir Frank Adcock, *Greek and Macedonian Kingship* (Cambridge University Press, 1953).
11. See Edwin O. Reischauer and John K. Fairbank, *East Asia: the Great Tradition* (Boston : Houghton Mifflin, 1960).
12. Karl A. Wittfogel, *Oriental Despotism: a Comparative Study of Total Power* (New Haven, Conn. : Yale University Press, 1957).
13. Mario Attilio Levi, *Political Power in the Ancient World* (Weidenfeld, 1965).

14. Sir Ernest Barker (ed.), *The Politics of Aristotle* (Oxford University Press, 1946).
15. Discussed in Werner Jaeger, *Paedia: the Ideals of Greek Culture* (Oxford University Press, 1939).
16. M. I. Finley, *The Ancient Greeks* (Pelican Books, 1966). See also W. G. Forrest, *The Emergence of Greek Democracy* (Weidenfeld, 1966).
17. J. R. Pole, *Political Representation in England and the Origins of the American Republic* (Macmillan, 1966).
18. Hannah Arendt, *The Human Condition*, Parts 1 and 2 (Cambridge University Press, 1958).
19. M. C. H. Finley, *Thucydides* (Cambridge, Mass. : Harvard University Press, 1942).
20. Leon Homo, *Roman Political Institutions*, 2nd ed. (Routledge, 1962).
21. Sir Frank Adcock, *Roman Political Ideas and Practice* (Ann Arbor : University of Michigan Press, 1959).
22. Sir Ronald Syme, *The Roman Revolution* (Oxford University Press, 1939).
23. A. H. M. Jones, *Studies in Roman Government and Law* (Oxford University Press, 1960).
24. C. N. Cochrane, *Christianity and Classical Culture* (Oxford University Press, 1957).
25. Cambridge Ancient History, Vol. X, *The Augustan Empire* (Cambridge University Press, 1934).
26. E. V. Arnold, *Roman Stoicism* (Cambridge University Press, 1911).
27. Plutarch, *Lives of the Noble Grecians and Romans* (Oxford : Blackwell, 1928).
28. Karl Marx, *Pre-Capitalist Economic Formations*, ed. Eric Hobsbawm (Lawrence & Wishart, 1964), although he is vague on the issue of oriental despotism. The *locus classicus* is, of course, Engels, *The Origin of the Family, Private Property and of the State* (various editions).
29. Karl Wittfogel, *Oriental Despotism: a Comparative Study of Total Power* (New Haven, Conn. : Yale University Press, 1957).
30. Barrington Moore, *Social Origins of Dictatorship and Democracy: Lord and Peasant in the Making of the Modern World* (Allen Lane, The Penguin Press, 1967).
31. Marc Bloch, *Feudal Society*, 2 vols. (Routledge, 1965).
32. Rushton Coulborn (ed.), *Feudalism in History* (Princeton, N.J. : Princeton University Press, 1956).

33. R. S. Rattray, *Ashanti Law and Constitution* (Oxford University Press, 1929).
34. Ivor Wilks, 'Ashanti Government', in Daryll Forde and P. M. Kaberry, *West African Kingdoms in the Nineteenth Century* (Oxford University Press, 1967).
35. Max Weber, *The Theory of Social and Economic Organisation*, ed. Talcott Parsons (Glencoe, Ill. : Free Press, 1957), first published in 1922 as Part One of *Wirtschaft und Gesellschaft*.
36. George L. Haskins, *The Growth of English Representative Government* (Oxford University Press, 1948).
37. Antonio Marongiu, *Medieval Parliaments: a Comparative Study* (Eyre & Spottiswoode, 1968).
38. A. R. Myers, 'Parliaments in Europe : the Representative Tradition', *History Today*, v (1955), 383–90, 446–54.
39. Bertie Wilkinson, *The Constitutional History of Medieval England, 1216–1399*, 3 vols. (Longmans, 1948–58).
40. Heinz Lubasz, ed., *The Development of the Modern State* (Collier-Macmillan, London 1964).
41. R. H. Tawney, *Religion and the Rise of Capitalism* (Murray, 1936).
42. G. R. Elton, *The Tudor Revolution in Government* (Cambridge University Press, 1953).
43. C. J. Friedrich, *The Age of the Baroque* (New York : Harper & Row, 1952).
44. Bernard Crick (ed.), *The Discourses of Machiavelli* (Pelican Classics, 1970).
45. Jean Bodin, *Six Books of the Commonwealth*, abridged and translated by M. J. Tooley (Oxford : Blackwell, 1967).
46. Friedrich Meinecke, *Machiavellism: the Doctrine of Raison d'État and its Place in Modern History* (Routledge, 1957).
47. J. W. Allen, *A History of Political Thought in the Sixteenth Century* (Methuen, 1928).
48. Max Weber, *The Theory of Social and Economic Organisation*, ed. Talcott Parsons (Collier-Macmillan, 1964).
49. Thomas Hobbes, *Leviathan*, edited and abridged with an introduction by John Plamenatz (Fontana, 1962).
50. Leslie Stephens, *The English Utilitarians*, Vol. I, and see Graham Wallas, 'Jeremy Bentham', *Political Science Quarterly*, March 1923, and his 'Bentham as a Political Inventor', *Contemporary Review*, March 1926.
51. Quoted by Charles McIlwain, *Constitutionalism Ancient and Modern*, revised ed. (Ithaca, N.Y. : Cornell University Press, 1947), p. 103.

52. Ibid., and J. G. A. Pocock, *The Ancient Constitution and the Feudal Law* (Cambridge University Press, 1957).
53. Peter Laslett (ed.), *Locke's Two Treatises on Government* (Cambridge University Press, 1963).
54. H. G. Königsberger and G. L. Moss, *Europe in the Sixteenth Century* (Longmans, 1968).
55. E. Kedourie, *Nationalism* (Hutchinson, 1961).
56. S. E. Finer, *Comparative Government* (Allen Lane, The Penguin Press, 1970), Part Four especially.
57. Ibid. and op. cit., chapter 9 of the same author's *The Man on Horseback* (Pall Mall Press, 1962), p. 243; and this author; *In Defence of Politics* (Penguin Books, 1964), chapter 3.
58. C. B. Macpherson, *The Real World of Democracy* (Oxford: Clarendon Press, 1966).
59. The whole body of post-war controversy and literature about the concept of 'totalitarianism' is so clearly and sensibly treated in Leonard Shapiro, *Totalitarianism* (Pall Mall and Macmillan, 1972). But perhaps also to note that the connection was seen even before the Second World War by four literary and political writers (that is, before academic writers like C. J. Friedrich and Hannah Arendt): Franz Borkenau, *The Spanish Cockpit*; Arthur Koestler, *Darkness at Noon*; George Orwell, *Homage to Catalonia*; and Ignazio Silone, *School for Dictators*.
60. As remarked by Hannah Arendt in her *The Origins of Totalitarianism*, 2nd ed. (Allen & Unwin, 1958).
61. Saint-Simon and Comte's advocacy of rule by a technocratic clerisy now seems so eccentric that we forget that in the early part of the century George Bernard Shaw is arguing much the same thing in *Man and Superman* and later H. G. Wells in *The Shape of Things to Come*. Few scientists advocate direct rule by scientists, but some very sane and eminent ones come very near, like Dennis Gabor in his recent *The Mature Society* (Secker & Warburg, 1971). Social Scientists, however, are less cautious. Harold Lasswell went through an elitist-scientific phase, as in his *Psychopathology and Politics* (1930), and the view is common among social scientists that, if not rulers, they should be the expert and privileged advisers to rulers (all that 'policy science' stuff). 'Technologism' is, in fact, a common doctrine with both a left-wing (Fabian) and a right-wing (managerial) variant (see my *In Defence of Politics*, chapter 5); but no good history of it has been written. However, W. H. G. Armytage's *Yesterdays Tomorrows: a Historical Survey of Future Societies* (Routledge, 1968) shows well the scientists' ambivalent,

redeeming/malevolent role in fiction, but not in non-fiction (though often the line is hard to draw).

62. Perhaps the most popular prophecy of doom was John Strachey's *The Coming Struggle for Power* (Gollancz, 1936). Analytically, however, see Krishan Kumar, *Revolution: The Theory and Practice of a European Idea* (Weidenfeld, 1971) and Hannah Arendt, *On Revolution* (Faber & Faber, 1963).

63. The old Social Democratic tradition can be seen best in its origins, in Edward Bernstein's first revisionist writings, and in its English form most clearly in R. H. Tawney's *Equality* (1931) and in his *Acquisitive Society* (1921). John Vaizey's brief *Social Democracy* (Weidenfeld, 1971) while wholly secondary, is a clear, readable introduction, far less parochial than its many competitors. J. A. Schumpeter's *Capitalism, Socialism and Democracy* (Allen & Unwin, 1943,) Karl Mannheim's *Freedom, Power and Democratic Planning* (Routledge, 1951) and Karl Popper's *The Open Society and its Enemies*, 2 vols., 4th ed. (Routledge, 1962) provide the often neglected theoretical underpinning for the 'inevitability of gradualness' thesis, more than – but also see – C. A. R. Crosland, *The Future of Socialism* (Cape, 1956).

64 The best general sketch of the political theory of science is Kingsley Amis, *New Maps of Hell* (Gollancz, 1961, but some useful points in W. H. G. Armytage, *Yesterdays Tomorrows*. Political theorists who dislike science-fiction should at least look at Isaac Asimov's work, particularly his trilogy, *The Foundation, Foundation and Empire*, and *The Second Foundation* (Panther Books) for symbols, myths and projections of modernity not found elsewhere.

65. James Burnham's *The Managerial Revolution* (Bloomington : Indiana University Press, 1960 – first published in 1941) is the *locus classicus* of this common assumption, although the convergence thesis finds explicit academic advocates less often than is supposed. (Daniel Bell's *The End of Ideology*, for instance, if actually read, has no implications in it for political or social convergence; perhaps on his own argument it should have, but it doesn't.) However, Clark Kerr, J. T. Dunlop, F. H. Harbisen and C. A. Myers, *Industrialism and Industrial Man* (Heinemann, 1963) can be fairly cited as an example (see the discussion and bibliography in E. G. Dunning and E. I. Hopper, 'Industrialism and the Problem of Convergence', *The Sociological Review*, July 1966, pp. 163–86 and also John H. Goldthorpe, 'Social Stratification in Industrial Society' in Paul

Halmos (ed.), *The Development of Industrial Societies* (*The Sociological Review*, Monograph No. 8, Keele 1964). And for a good critique of both academic and popular versions, Raymond Aron, *The Industrial Society* (Weidenfeld, 1967).

66. Again the uniqueness of the Third World is a common view in political and newpaper rhetoric but is more hard to pin down in books. Kwesi Armah, *Africa's Golden Road* (Heinemann, 1965) could be looked at as exemplary. Peter Worsley, *The Third World* (Weidenfeld, 1964) is a moderate statement of the thesis. Ernest Gellner's *Thought and Change* (Weidenfeld, 1964) and his 'Democracy and Industrialisation', *Archives of European Sociology*, VIII (1967) 47–79, raise the fundamental problems.

67. E. Kedourie, *Nationalism* (Hutchinson, 1964), and B. Akzin, *State and Nation* (Hutchinson, 1964).

68. James Joll, *The Anarchist* (Eyre & Spottiswoode, 1964) and David E. Apter and James Joll (eds.), *Anarchism Today* (Macmillan, 1971).

69. Machiavelli's *Discourses* is really the *locus classicus* of the 'role of the people' theory, since all depends on whether the people have *virtu* (or civic spirit) or not. The great white elephant of our times, Gabriel Almond and Sidney Verba, *The Civic Culture* (Boston : Little, Brown, 1965), seeks to test the importance of a civic culture for stability, but both the criteria and the conclusions are muddled. Generally the theory is held politically by European radicals (in the Left-Liberal sense), and morally appears to be the assumption that might rescue most election studies from triviality, or at least from such disproportionate effort.

70. Most of traditional political thought assumes the importance of right reason in the maintenance of order, occasionally a manipulative argument is developed, as in Machiavelli's bitter attacks on the Church in *The Prince* for subverting civic virtue and his praise of the pagan religion of Rome, and in Mandeville's *Inquiry into the Origin of Honour and the Usefulness of Christianity in War* (1732).

Most studies of authority patterns and legitimation, even Weber's, make this assumption, so do studies of the importance of propaganda and of 'necessary beliefs' of political myths.

71. All Marxists and most sociologists hold this view – though with the latter the qualifications are usually as important as the formal adherence. But there is a conservative version also, turning upon myths or perceptions of natural hierarchy.

72. Gaetano Mosca's *The Ruling Class* (New York : McGraw-Hill,

94

1939) (originally published in 1896 as *Elementi di Scienza Politica*) is the classic statement, together with Vilfredo Pareto's *Les Systemes Socialistes*, 2 vols. (Giard, Paris, 1902–3). But all writings on the power of aristocracies have to be seen in this context, even before the modern sociological-analytical studies for elites, for which we see T. B. Bottomore, *Elites and Society* (Watts, 1964) and Geraint Parry, *Political Elites* (Allen & Unwin, 1969).

73. The institutional school only appears plausible when the importance of political doctrines as sources of stability is questioned, or rather when one of them gains ascendancy over the others, the belief in 'constitutional government'. The believe that if you get institutions right all else follows is found at its crudest in James Bryce, *Modern Democracies* and in its most subtle form in Carl J. Friedrich, *Constitutional Government and Democracy* (New York : Harper & Row, 1937) and many subsequent editions. J. S. Mill's *Representative Government* (1861) is perhaps the finest synthesis of the doctrinal and the institutional school. Studies of comparative institutions are still made as if they mean something in themselves, see Leslie Wolf-Phillips, *Comparative Constitutions,* in this series (1972) : so the school is not quite dead.

74. The type of economy is obviously seen as the key by, once again, all Marxists, but also by most liberal economists, see F. A. Hayek's *Individualism and Economic Order* (Routledge, 1949) and his *The Constitution of Liberty* (Routledge, 1960).

75. Most Marxists see property as the key, but the view is rendered purely formal or largely meaningless by failure to distinguish between ownership and control, as shown so well in Ralf Dahrendorf, *Class and Class Conflict in an Industrial Society* (Routledge, 1959). Far more subtle attempts to differentiate between the political consequences of forms of land tenure are to be found in Sir Henry Maine, *Ancient Law,* with notes by Sir Frederick Pollock (John Murray, 1906), in Karl Wittfogel, *Oriental Despotism,* and Barrington Moore, *Social Origins of Dictatorship and Democracy.*

76. The literature is vast of those who believe that if individuals or groups themselves decide whether or not to obey the law, then social order is endangered (thus that law determines morality). Thomas Hobbes in the seventeenth century and Hans Kelsen actually in the twentieth century are the great advocates of this position. But the most subtle advocacy is still in A. V. Dicey, *Law of the Constitution* (Macmillan, 1885) and his Lectures on the *Relation between Law and Public Opinion in England*

During the Nineteenth Century, 2nd ed. (Macmillan, 1905).

77. Hegel's overriding assumption that the state must embody philosophic truth to be stable and just, see vol. 3 of *Hegel's Lectures on the History of Philosophy*, edited and translated by E. S. Haldane and Frances H. Simson (Routledge, 1896; reprinted 1955 and 1963), but also, equally, Sir Karl Popper's famous attempt to show a unique fit between the epistemology of scientific method and liberal-democracy, *The Open Society and Its Enemies*, 2 vols. (Routledge, 1945).

78. There is a huge and great popular literature on the freedom of the press in republics and on censorship in autocracies, and now more sophisticated stuff on communications theory. One might cite Milton's *Areopagitica*, Mill's *On Liberty* and, more doubtfully, Karl W. Deutsch's *The Nerves of Government: Models of Communication and Control* (Glencoe, Ill. : Free Press, 1963). Discount the anti-God obsession (they plainly believed in him, but disliked him), then much of the late-nineteenth-century rationalist, free-thought literature makes the same point.

79. Again a vast literature, both popular and academic, which maintains that the existence of open political dispute is the hallmark of a stable and free society. 'Conflict theorists' are more relevant here than 'consensus theorists' who more properly belong in the doctrinal school (see note 70 above). But who dares to say who since Aristotle are the masters of this school or the contemporary disciples? The journal *Government and Opposition* in contemporary political studies seems clearest in its tempered adherence to this view.